THE MAKING
OF A MISSIONARY

THE MAKING
OF A MISSIONARY

Joseph L. Bishop

BOOKCRAFT, INC.
Salt Lake City, Utah

Library of Congress Catalog Card Number: 81-71756
ISBN O-88494-451-4

3 4 5 6 7 8 9 10   89 88 87 86 85

Lithographed in the United States of America
PUBLISHERS PRESS
Salt Lake City, Utah

To my father and mother, J. Layton and Fontella Bishop;
to my wife, Carolyn;
and my five sons, Gregory, Robert, Michael, Steven, and Scott
—for all are outstanding missionaries

Contents

Preface

The Lord's work is a work of order. In it harmony prevails, each of its elements doing what it was assigned according to a holy schedule. If our work is to reflect the spirit and will of our divine Father, harmony must exist in our missionary endeavors.

Consistently, there are stages of development for missionaries. Each step is preparatory to the next—each exists in total concord with the others, and each step is made in sequence so as not to disrupt the agreement and order of the Lord's plan. This book focuses on the identification of the elements, their order (sequence of events), and their relationship with one another.

The book does not treat specific mission programs. To do so would suggest that all missions should subscribe to one program, whereas no two missions can be alike. Rather, the intent is to focus on those divine principles which are basic to the success of the missionary regardless of where he serves; to establish a semblance of order as to which things might appropriately be considered first, then second, etc.; and to demonstrate the relationship of these elements one with another.

The treatment is limited. It reflects only those elements which experience has demonstrated as being of significant consequence, frequently misunderstood, or overlooked. Indeed, it provides merely a simple point of departure for those who would continue to inquire of the Lord. He is the fountain of all inspiration. These materials will only assist the missionary in preparing to drink from that fountain. If he prepares well, he may drink deeply and be eternally rewarded.

The names of the missionaries used in the book have been changed. The examples, however, are taken from true missionary experiences and accurately reflect life in the mission field.

Acknowledgments

While I alone am responsible for the contents of this book, many others assisted directly or indirectly by their contributions to my life and learning in the missionary experience.

I give thanks to my dear friend Nathan C. Tanner for his example of love and Christlike concern while we served in the mission field.

I acknowledge with appreciation the contribution of the outstanding missionaries I was privileged to preside over in the Argentina Buenos Aires North Mission, whose dedication, love, and service were fundamental in the preparation of this book. I particularly appreciate the kind and faithful assistance of Martin Gwynn and William Slater in typing, retyping, and editing the manuscript.

I express gratitude, love, and admiration to my mentor, Elder Robert E. Wells, a great missionary who uncovered to my view the eternal principles of missionary work expressed in this book.

Finally I express boundless and eternal indebtedness to our Heavenly Father, not least for the glimpses I have received of his glorious work.

Introduction

The suggestions and principles contained in this book are based upon the eternal truth that all blessings are predicated upon laws. The faithful missionary will seek undauntedly for an understanding of those laws and conditions which will open the door to the conversion of souls unto the Lord.

The correct identification of such laws and conditions is not a process of intellectualization; rather, it is a process of being guided by the Spirit to such understanding. The purpose of this book is to focus on examples of different conditions of the law and thus serve as a point of departure in assisting the reader, through his worthiness, to receive additional light and knowledge from on high.

To receive a blessing, one must both abide in the law and fulfill its conditions. "For all who will have a blessing at my hands shall abide the law which was appointed for that blessing, *and the conditions* thereof, as were instituted from before the foundation of the world." (D&C 132:5; emphasis added.) The conditions of the law define, set forth, clarify, and in other ways establish the law's own identity and independence. Thus, to understand clearly any of God's laws, one must also understand all of the accompanying conditions of that law.

> Once a law has been ordained, it thereafter operates automatically; that is, whenever there is compliance with its terms and conditions, the promised results accrue. (Bruce R. McConkie, *Mormon Doctrine*, 2nd ed. [Salt Lake City: Bookcraft, Inc., 1966], p. 433.)

Clearly, deviation from the conditions of a law of God is deviation from that law, and deviation from the law cuts off its promised blessings. Similarly, compliance with the conditions of a law is compliance with that law, and it assures the promised blessings. A knowledge and understanding of the conditions of the law, as well as of the law itself, can come only through the Light of Christ, by which all things are governed (D&C 88:13); or, for a Church member, through the Holy Ghost. The importance of seeking and gaining the Spirit cannot be overemphasized in the search for missionary success.

My sincere prayer is that, through the sharing of my cherished missionary experiences, however limited they may be, the Spirit may testify to the reader's soul of those conditions and laws which may be of the most value to him in his own missionary work, and that this book may thus assist in the making of a missionary.

SECTION 1

Principles
of
Personal Worthiness

A mission is much like a "mini" life. The missionary arrives in the mission field incapable of doing much without the loving care of mission "parents" and particularly of companions. In missions wherein the language is not the missionary's native tongue his dependence on others is even more pronounced.

As the missionary grows into mission "adolescence," he learns to organize the day-to-day missionary work but is not yet able to cope with the intricate or unexpected events of missionary disappointments. Soon the missionary becomes experienced enough to assist others as he becomes senior companion, district leader, zone leader, etc. He enjoys his "middle age" of experience and the comfort of knowing how to function properly. Finally, the maturity of "advanced age" comes upon him as he is identified by all as one of the "old" missionaries. Soon he passes from the life of a full-time mission to return to that world he knew before.

That "passing" is one of peace and contentment if the missionary can look back at his labors with the knowledge of having done his best and having prepared himself well for the start of his own "creation."

The foundation of his success throughout his mission, his mini-life, as he progresses through each of the previously described phases, is personal worthiness. There is no other substitute. Of all requisites to successful missionary work, none is more important or necessary than personal worthiness. If a missionary is not worthy, he cannot perform an effective mission.

Personal worthiness is active, not passive. It is dynamic, not static. It is proven with each extra-mile sprint. It gains momentum with each individual personal sacrifice. It grows with each desire of the missionary to prove his worth.

No mission program, no plan, and no secret formula will replace the Lord's direct blessings. And those blessings are not forthcoming if the missionary is not worthy. Worthiness is the base upon which all other talents and efforts are erected. To properly find the Lord's elect, one must be worthy. To teach or baptize, one must be worthy. There is no substitute for this condition of God's law.

To be called as an official representative of the Lord Jesus Christ and to cry repentance to those who are becoming ripe in iniquity is indeed a sobering responsibility. Often the recently called missionary cannot fully rejoice in his calling, as he still feels unworthy.

For the missionary, worthiness involves at least seven categories of personal effort:

1. Proper confession.
2. Thought control.
3. Obedience.
4. Observance of mission rules.
5. Faithfulness to the Lord.
6. Pure motives.
7. Personal sacrifice.

The list is not all-inclusive; other areas will occur to the reader.

Each category contains basic principles of the Lord's laws. Obedience to these laws and their conditions will result in sound progression toward personal worthiness.

Chapter 1

Proper Confession

The task at hand is not to enumerate the long list of "don'ts" or "thou shalt nots." The point is simple and direct: Representatives of the Lord are commanded to obtain the Spirit before teaching the gospel. The unrepentant missionary cannot have the Spirit. His unworthiness nullifies his prayer of faith.

> And the Spirit shall be given unto you by the prayer of faith; and if ye receive not the Spirit ye shall not teach. (D&C 42:14.)

To be the Lord's representative, one must first be totally clean. While the subject of repentance is not new, the process contained therein is not always understood. The formula is straightforward and candid:

> To gain forgiveness through repentance a person must have a conviction of guilt, a godly sorrow for his sin, and a contrite spirit. He must desire to be relieved of the burden of sin, have a fixed determination to forsake his evil ways, *be willing to confess his sins,* and forgive those who have trespassed against him; he must accept the cleansing power of the blood of Christ. (Bruce R. McConkie, *Mormon Doctrine,* 2nd ed. [Salt Lake City: Bookcraft, Inc., 1966], p. 630; emphasis added.)

The segment which is often misunderstood in the repentance process is proper confession. Countless missionaries have unsuccessfully tried to bypass that all-important step in their ladder to heavenly forgiveness. Rather than confess, many try desperately to work out their sins in the mission field. They work longer, they try harder, and they pray more diligently, but they fail to recognize the conditions of the law of repentance.

God cannot break his own law or bypass any of the conditions it contains. The condition of confession for grievous sins cannot be ignored. If a bishop fails to ask the prospective missionary the right questions, the missionary has the obligation to bring fully to light any suspect sins. This process is not to humiliate the sinner—it is to unburden him. It relieves him of the terrible guilt and feelings of despair. It helps to produce a contrite spirit—proof to the Lord of a person's sincerity. Without that offering, the Lord's divine process is short-circuited. By virtue of the conditions of the law he cannot extend his forgiveness.

Since the process of confession is to unburden and make new, why is there reluctance on the part of the sinner in complying with that condition of the law? It is because Satan would have him believe that the shame of the sin is so great that he must do everything in his power to hide his error. But the truth is the exact opposite. The authorized leader who listens to the confession does not focus on the shame of the sin. His attention is directed squarely on the growth of the individual.

> Behold, he who has repented of his sins, the same is forgiven, and I, the Lord remember them no more. (D&C 58:42.)

On one occasion a missionary said to me, "President, do you remember what I told you in our last interview?" I was at a total loss. What was it he had said? I could not remember, regardless of how hard I tried.

Feeling somewhat ashamed, I answered, "I'm sorry, Elder. No, I don't remember. What was it?"

His eyes lighted up and his countenance brightened. "You really can't remember?" he quizzed.

"No," I answered, still not understanding the impact that my lack of memory was having upon him.

He hastily replied, "That's great, President! I just wanted you to know that I'm doing fine—just fine!"

To this day I do not remember what sin that elder confessed to me. I will always remember, however, what a great missionary he was. He was one of the most outstanding zone leaders I was privileged to work with. He was not called to be a missionary for what he was, nor is anyone else; rather, he was called to become a defender of the truth—one who is not afraid to proclaim the restored gospel of Jesus Christ. In part he was called to repent of his sins, and that is precisely what he did. The Lord said: "For I will forgive you of your sins with this commandment—that you remain steadfast in your minds in solemnity and the spirit of prayer, *in bearing testimony to all the world* of those things which are communicated to you." (D&C 84:61; emphasis added.)

That great zone leader bore testimony to all who would listen. I know his heart, and I know of his sincerity; yet I no longer know his sins, because after they were confessed I no longer remembered them. That troubles me not, for the Lord no longer remembers them either. And as far as possible the repentant sinner should forget his confessed sins. Satan often attempts to bring to the mind of the missionary his past sins to make him feel unworthy to carry forth the gospel message. If his sins have been taken care of through the appropriate priesthood leader, then that missionary may disregard the entire issue. If the thought arises, he should say to himself, *I know where that thought is coming from. It is Satan hard at work.* Then he should literally force that negative element from his mind.

The following case will illustrate the importance of immediate confession of grievous sins:

Elder Green was a hard-working missionary. Each month he would review with me his efforts for the month. His goals were high but were purely "activity" goals; that is, he always listed such items as the number of hours he planned to work or the number of houses he was going to visit, and so on. It soon became obvious that he was afraid to establish meaningful goals (goals relative to the number of baptisms, the number of weekly discussions, or the number of investigators he wanted to have attending church the following Sunday). Week after week he trumpeted how hard he was working without success. "The people never let us in," he bemoaned; or he would write, "The area is totally 'burned out.'" Yet other missionaries would find success a few days later in the same area that he had labeled "Area Impossible."

I reviewed with him his lack of success. Clearly, the problem was either his inability to find and teach the Lord's elect or his lack of personal worthiness. After some probing questions, the real problem finally surfaced. That missionary had committed a very serious moral sin prior to entering the mission field. Because of his shame, he had never confessed it. Each step in the mission process added more to the burden of guilt upon him. He was not worthy to enter the temple, but he felt that he had gone too far to retreat. Now he was in the mission field trying to be true to his calling. He worried that if anyone found out he would be sent home to his own disgrace and that of friends and family. His only recourse, he resolved, was to remain silent and to endeavor to work out his forgiveness with the Lord. He worked hard, but he knew that he was unworthy of the Spirit. Thus he became discouraged, negative, and argumentative. Externally he was pushing himself to demonstrate to the Lord, his mission president, and his companion that he was a hard worker. Deep inside, however, his heart was breaking.

Once he confessed his sin, his rehabilitation began and he found relief. After appropriate correspondence with his bishop and stake president, he was able to remain in the mission field and complete an honorable mission.

After the burden of guilt was lifted, that elder found the Lord. Overnight his work became directed toward baptisms, and he became a totally different missionary. After he had proved himself worthy, the blessings came forth and he was successful. He terminated his mission being the missionary he had dreamed of.

But he had lost nearly a year of work by failure to confess his sin more promptly. He had sought diligently to cover up the sin with his hard work. He had failed to understand that work is not the first prerequisite to missionary success. The required element is, and always will be in the Lord's kingdom, personal worthiness.

Chapter 2

Thought Control

The main difference between the divine creation of man and that of the animal is man's intellect. His ability to design his destiny by reason, deduction, and evaluation of the consequences of his actions has established his superiority. Logically, if man fails to consider the consequences of his actions by allowing his thoughts to run uncontrolled, he will inevitably descend nearer to the level of the animals and will reap the rewards of carnality. When wicked thoughts direct his actions, man departs from the spiritual and becomes sensual, devilish, and an enemy to God (Moses 6:49). The focal point rests upon man's ability to control that God-given intellect and to direct his thoughts. His thoughts, in turn, can direct his actions so that they are compatible with the Lord's plan for the individual's divine destiny.

It seems strange that there are missionaries who embark in the service of their Lord assuming there is little relationship between their thoughts and their worthiness to have the Spirit. On one occasion, Elder Jones took liberties with his thoughts, rationalizing that because he took no action on them they were harmless. He described it in the following manner:

"We had just finished a beautiful baptism. The day was sunny, the birds were singing in the trees, and I felt good all over. We were in a member's car waiting to take our newly baptized family to their home. My companion was in the front seat chatting with Brother Thompson, and I was alone in the back.

"Because the day was so beautiful, I allowed my thoughts to drift to my home. I remembered the parties we used to have at the beach on such sunny days and some of the girls I used to date. At that point I rationalized that I would indulge myself in some 'wild daydreaming.' After all, I was in a car with my companion and hardly anything could go wrong. I was totally protected—I thought. My thoughts were not uplifting. In fact, they were really terrible. I opened the floodgates to all the things of the world that Satan wanted me to imagine were happening to me. It was really bad.

"When our newly baptized family arrived at the car for their ride home, I felt a profound sense of guilt. They literally glowed with spirituality. Although I was the one who had baptized them, I felt unworthy to be in their presence. I felt very guilty for my terrible thoughts."

Elder Jones was unable to continue functioning as a representative of the Lord until he had unburdened his soul in confession to his mission president and had once again reestablished his relationship with his Savior. The Spirit was not with him, and he wasted several precious days of missionary work. He *did* nothing wrong, he only *thought* wrong thoughts. But in that instant he became a "natural man" (Mosiah 3:19). He was no longer spiritual, and he was no longer powerful. He was no longer a true representative of the Lord Jesus Christ. He remained that way until he complied with the Spirit. The Lord said:

> This I say then, Walk in the Spirit, and ye shall not fulfil the lust of the flesh.
> For the flesh lusteth against the Spirit, and the Spirit against the flesh: and these are contrary the one to the other: so that ye cannot do the things that ye would. (Galatians 5:16-17.)

A mission president was traveling by commuter train to his office. As the train filled to overflowing with rush-hour traffic, he found himself pushed face to face against a very attractive young woman. Try as he might, there was no room to avoid physical contact. The president was caught with one arm pinned to his side while the other, bent at an angle, held his Book of Mormon close to his face.

Recognizing the inappropriateness of the situation and his inability to change it, he could only turn his thoughts inward. He closed his eyes, offered up a prayer, and then read and reread the opened pages of his Book of Mormon which were pressed almost to his face.

During the hour-long ride to the city, he had no inappropriate thoughts. He wrapped himself up in a spiritual experience and meditated different passages in the Book of Mormon. He imagined how the Saints must have felt as Christ appeared to them on the American continent. He imagined himself a participant in that scene. He conjured to mind the humility that Nephi must have felt as he was called forth by Christ himself. He visualized the joy that must have been Nephi's (3 Nephi 11:17-21).

There was no temptation for that president. There was no gigantic trial. He had controlled his thoughts. That expression of self-discipline, as individually small as it may have been, was powerful enough to totally protect him from what might have been potential danger. There is virtually no normal situation conjured by Satan which cannot be defused by the simple practice of thought control.

The train arrived at its destination, and its hordes of people began to pour forth. The president looked up from his reading and pondering into the smiling faces of two missionaries. They had been watching the entire episode from only a few feet away. As they departed with the crowd, each waved a tract at the president to let him know that his example had been noticed and copied. They too had pulled their spiritual "security blankets" tightly around their minds and had arrived unscathed.

The Savior said:

> Ye have heard that it was said by them of old time, Thou shalt not commit adultery:
> But I say unto you, That whosoever looketh on a woman to lust after her hath committed adultery with her already in his heart. (Matthew 5:27-28.)

In rehearsing the same issue as recorded in Doctrine and

Covenants 63:16, the Lord added, referring to those that lust, "they shall not have the Spirit, but shall deny the faith and shall fear."

The Savior has repeatedly admonished his Saints to control their thoughts.

> Abstain from fleshly lusts, which war against the soul. (1 Peter 2:11.)

> Cease . . . from all your lustful desires. (D&C 88:121.)

> For all that is in the world, the lust of the flesh, and the lust of the eyes, and the pride of life, is not of the Father, but is of the world.
> And the world passeth away, and the lust thereof: but he that doeth the will of God abideth for ever. (1 John 2:16-17.)

Ronald Loveland, former president of the Texas San Antonio Mission, tells of traveling with one of his missionaries to a zone conference. President Loveland was aware that at a particular juncture in the road there was a large highway sign advertising a dubious product. As is all too common, the advertisement featured an immodestly dressed young woman in a seductive pose. President Loveland wondered how his young missionary might respond to that event. He reports that as they turned the corner in full view of the advertisement, the missionary immediately shifted in his seat, positioning his body at an angle away from the sign. He turned his head away from that view and began to talk to President Loveland. He continued swivelling away from the sign, with his head always facing away until they had passed by the sign.

That missionary understood the subtle dangers of allowing the windows of his soul to view something which could trigger the mind to wrong thoughts. He merely refused to be tempted. Satan with that suggestive scene had absolutely no power over that missionary. Not one word was ever said about the incident, but President Loveland made a mental note: Here was a missionary who could be trusted. Here was a missionary who understood that a small amount of self-discipline is a dramatically powerful defense against Satan and his temptations.

The response can be automatic. If a view is offensive to the soul, merely close the eyelids. If a sound irritates the spirit, replace it in the mind by thinking of an uplifting song, reviewing a favorite scripture, or using any other weapon to seal up the fortress and keep Satan out. The power is in us, if we but use it wisely, to help ourselves and to help others. The Lord's promise to those who "commit" their works unto him is power to control and establish their thoughts (Proverbs 16:3). The promise is extended; missionaries need only to obey. The faithful will reap the Lord's protection and will experience the success he holds in store for them.

Chapter 3

Obedience

Power, dominion, and authority over the adversary come only when one learns to obey. By the simple act of obedience, extensive authority over the tempter's snare is given to him who is true.

If missionaries are to be led line upon line, precept upon precept, if they are to have the power of faith and discernment to recognize the Lord's elect, if blessings and other things which they may righteously desire are to be theirs, they must search out the laws upon which the desired blessings are founded and obey them.

> Obedience is the first law of heaven, the cornerstone upon which all righteousness and progression rest. It consists in compliance with divine law, in conformity to the mind and will of Deity, in complete subjection to God and his commands. (*Mormon Doctrine*, p. 539.)

The holy scriptures are full of examples of those who have refused to obey. The most rebellious, the father of all lies, is Satan. He presented to the holy council his plan which would force all men to obey God's commandments during their earthly estate. He promised that all would be saved. But in return he required that God grant him His power. Satan's plan was rejected because it failed to comply with the principle of free agency and because his motives were impure. Thus he "was angry, and kept not his first estate; and, at that day, many followed after him." (Abraham 3:28.)

Those who followed agreed with Satan's plans. They too wanted God's power and wanted to possess all things. They too rebelled.

That account might lead some to believe that the Lord does not want his children to have power or great possessions. To the contrary, he desires that his children receive "all that [the] Father hath" (D&C 84:38), but to do so they must first learn to use their God-given power in an appropriate manner. He has to be assured that they will be responsible and use their gifts in building and fortifying others and not in exercising unrighteous dominion over them. That is why these godly powers are reserved for those who have proven themselves before him through obedience to his commandments. He has said:

> He that is ordained of God and sent forth, the same is appointed to be the greatest, notwithstanding he is the least and the servant of all.
>
> Wherefore, *he is possessor of all things; for all things are subject unto him*, both in heaven and on earth, the life and the light, the Spirit and the power, sent forth by the will of the Father through Jesus Christ, his Son. (D&C 50:26-27; emphasis added.)

To be the "possessor of all things" and to be entrusted with power over "all things, both in heaven and on earth," one must be worthy of the responsibility. God's blessings are attached to his laws. He who learns to obey the law receives the blessing.

> There is a law, irrevocably decreed in heaven before the foundations of this world, upon which all blessings are predicated—
>
> And when we obtain any blessing from God, it is by obedience to that law upon which it is predicated. (D&C 130:20-21.)

Those who rebel against God's authority have not learned that power, dominion, and authority are available only to those who would use such resources in a righteous, unselfish manner. The basis of all sin is selfishness. He who is selfish cannot be trusted with the Lord's possessions. To receive the Lord's blessings, one must be free of sin:

> But no man is possessor of all things except he be purified and cleansed from all sin.

And if ye are purified and cleansed from all sin, ye shall ask whatsoever you will in the name of Jesus and it shall be done. (D&C 50:28-29.)

The Lord's gift of eternal life and exaltation to the obedient, the ultimate possession of all things, is beyond mortal comprehension or imagination.

The missionary who is obedient to God's laws will receive God's blessings. But what are God's laws? They are infinite. There are those laws which are designed for the temporal salvation of all Church members in the last days:

Given for a principle with promise, adapted to the capacity of the weak and the weakest of all saints, who are or can be called saints. (D&C 89:3.)

There are higher laws which progressively require a higher level of understanding and obedience. The greater the understanding, the greater the obedience and the greater the blessings. That progression will bring the faithful to dwell with their Maker someday, having been tried and proven in all things.

The missionary must learn to understand the whisperings of the Spirit and obey. He must arrive at the point of going beyond the written mission rules, for while he continues to obey all those rules he graduates to a higher level of obedience. These "higher" laws are not so obvious, nor do they apply to all missionaries. The Spirit may direct one missionary to obey a special, higher set of rules and regulations. They are not generalizable.

The Spirit of the Lord simply whispers softly and directly to the individual. These holy promptings will at times be received while the missionary is engaged in doing that which the Spirit will declare as inappropriate. He will sense fleeting pangs of guilt or uneasiness. Many times these promptings are so subtle that the missionary may be tempted to dismiss them as random thoughts. The law of free agency precludes the Holy Spirit from forcing man to pay attention and do his will. He can only softly call. It is left to the missionary to learn to "listen," identify, and obey these promptings.

The question arises: How can we know if that which we are receiving is the prompting of the Spirit or if we are experiencing a fleeting random thought or even promptings of the evil one? The answer is clear. We simply need to ask. Alma said, "Counsel with the Lord in all thy doings and he will direct thee for good." (Alma 37:37.) Joseph Smith was told, "Ask, and ye shall receive; knock and it shall be opened unto you." (D&C 4:7.) The humble missionary can receive direct confirmation through the promptings of the Spirit. The Lord instructed Oliver Cowdery on these principles. He said: "But if it be not right you shall have no such feelings, but you shall have a stupor of thought that shall cause you to forget the thing which is wrong." (D&C 9:9.)

The Lord will instruct us in the same fashion. But we must "listen," discern, and then obey. These gifts are not given all at once. Each is earned one by one. As we correctly respond to the Lord's promptings, more are given, until finally one day we will walk with Almighty God.

The great gift of the Spirit is the much-desired reward for the faithful and obedient. The missionary who fails to understand this divine law and reluctantly obeys a mission rule out of obligation or peer pressure will only be blessed according to the level of his sacrifice. How much greater his joy and blessings would be if he were to understand the principle of the law! To learn not only to obey but also to love to obey are two great opportunities awaiting all missionaries who serve faithfully. Through proper obedience to the Lord's commandments, worthy missionaries can call forth the blessings which await them.

As the missionary experiences more and more blessings because of his obedience, he will witness more and more the Lord's hand in all that he does. As he progresses in his obedience, more principles of truth will be revealed to him and he will be given more power to aid him in the ministry. He will labor with authority and dominion over all things according to the blessing given to him as he becomes a mighty servant of the Lord. Seek to obey, and it shall be given unto you.

Chapter 4

Observance of Mission Rules

There are rules which apply to all missions and there are those unique rules which have reference to only one specific mission or missionary. However, there are no mission rules which exist for the sole purpose of teaching discipline. The mission is not the army.

Rules exist for two major reasons: to protect the missionary from physical and spiritual harm and to help him be successful. For example, the Church rule is that missionaries travel two by two. The Savior provided the foundation for that rule in this dispensation when he said: "And let them journey together, or two by two, as seemeth them good." (D&C 61:35.)

The Lord also said: "And if any man among you be strong in the Spirit, let him take with him him that is weak, that he may be edified in all meekness, that he may become strong also." (D&C 84:106.) Missionaries often attribute their success to special companions who lift them to new heights and expose them to new insights into the gospel principles. How meaningful to the individual is the Lord's commandment to send missionaries two by two so that the weak might be edified and lifted up! That rule insures protection and provokes success. Success, of course, brings happiness.

The mission rule of traveling and teaching two by two is to be considered more than a mission rule. Its roots come from the "law of witnesses" which the Lord ordained: "In the mouth of two or three witnesses shall every word be established." (2 Corinthians 13:1. See also Deuteronomy 17:6; 19:15; Matthew 18:16; John 8:12-29.)

Elder Bruce R. McConkie affirms the same principle for this dispensation:

> Never does one man stand alone in establishing a new dispensation of revealed truth, or in carrying the burden of such a message and warning to the world. In every dispensation, from Adam to the present, two or more witnesses have always joined their testimonies, thus leaving their hearers without excuse in the day of judgment should the testimony be rejected. (*Mormon Doctrine*, p. 436.)

The Lord's law of witnesses provides protection to all who heed its counsel. By the same logic, when the law is broken the protection is lost. To illustrate that point, I refer to a tragic incident as related by Elder Marvin J. Ashton at the Mission Presidents Seminar held in Montevideo, Uruguay, November 1980. Elder Black and his companion returned home late one evening. They were exhausted. They had been out all day long in the hot sun going from door to door without seeing one friendly face. No one invited them in, and no one extended a hand of fellowship in their direction. Door after door was rudely slammed in their faces.

They were poking around in the kitchen trying to stir up something simple to eat, and they found that they needed some milk. The senior companion suggested that he would start to prepare the meal if Elder Black would run down to the corner store, only one block away, to buy a quart of milk.

As Elder Black reluctantly made his way to the store, his errand was interrupted by a pretty girl about his age standing in the doorway of her apartment. It was the first time in the entire day that anyone had even spoken to him in a half-friendly way. He gladly stopped to talk to her. After chatting for a few minutes, she invited him in. It wasn't until after he had committed serious sin that he realized that the apartment had recently been rented as a new illicit massage parlor and that the pretty girl was just working to establish a new clientele.

After Elder Black left her apartment, he went directly back to his companion and told him what had happened. The next day he met with his mission president and informed him of the misadventure. The following day Elder Black was excommunicated from the Church and sent home.

The missionary had no planned escapade in mind when he went for milk. He had no intention of committing such a grievous sin. But he and his protection had been separated. Had his companion been with him, he would have been safe. He would not have fallen.

Satan works cleverly and diligently to ensnare the Lord's workers. The battle is real. He and his helpers exist. Missionaries must always be prepared to meet any eventuality. Those eventualities have virtually all been considered and are reflected in mission rules. *No missionary has ever fallen from grace in the mission field without having broken some mission rule.* Few dangerous situations could ever develop if missionaries would but diligently follow the rules which are designed to offer the necessary protection.

The mission president is responsible to modify rules which are not applicable to his mission because of local customs and so forth. For example, the missionary manual suggests that missionaries be in their beds by 10:30 P.M. In some South American countries during the summer months it is not uncommon to see little children playing in the streets even at midnight. The custom is to sleep during the heat of the day (a practice commonly referred to as the *siesta*) and retire to bed at night much later than the normal time. In those countries the missionaries' work schedules are designed to be compatible with the customs of the country. If missionaries were to work in the early afternoon, according to the suggested universal time, they probably would create more enemies than converts. The point is simple: Rules are to be adapted to local conditions, but it is the mission president who is to make that adaptation, not the missionary.

Occasionally a rule may exist which will not be understood by all missionaries. If the missionary has reached a level of understanding and obedience equal to his calling, he will accept and keep the mission rules without further question. He will have complete faith that there is valid reason for their existence in every instance. An example of this kind of obedience is found in the writings of Moses. It refers to the specific commandment which the Lord gave to Adam and Eve:

> And he gave unto them commandments, that they should worship the Lord their God, and should offer the firstlings of their flocks, for an offering unto the Lord. And Adam was obedient unto the commandments of the Lord.
> And after many days an angel of the Lord appeared unto Adam saying: Why dost thou offer sacrifices unto the Lord? And Adam said unto him: I know not, save the Lord commanded me. (Moses 5:5-6.)

If missionaries are to grow to the level of perfect trust and faith so that someday they can say, as did Adam, "I know not, save the Lord commanded me," it would seem appropriate to further that process in the mission field. By learning to obey minor rules and regulations they will prepare themselves to accept all things the Lord would have them do. The following true story illustrates this point:

Sister Fernandez complained that she saw absolutely no benefit in the mission rule of listening to music only on preparation day, and then only music which was approved by the mission as being uplifting. She rebelliously continued to ignore the mission rule by playing her cassette tapes whenever she pleased. Her actions caused contention between her and the other three sisters who lived with her. Finally, the problem grew in proportion and the mission president was brought into it.

The president patiently explained the purpose of the rule to her: Missionaries are called to find the Lord's elect and teach them the principles of the gospel. The key factor in that process is to be able to discern who the elect are. The worthy missionary who is continually praying for that divine help will receive it—if there is no interference. If music is playing in the background, if a melody is cycling through the mind, that missionary will be distracted from receiving the whisperings of the Spirit. Missionaries are to study, pray, and ponder. Pondering divine truths cannot take place if music is playing. Clearly, little inspiration can enter the mind if a song is already occupying that space.

Once Sister Fernandez finally understood the purpose of the rule, she adjusted accordingly and the problem was solved. However, would it not have been better for her to keep the rule and to ask her mission president for clarification of it rather than to simply break it? Was it appropriate for her to rebel because of her lack of understanding? Would it not have been best for her to sacrifice her selfish desire for the benefit of the other missionaries? Would it not have been appropriate for her to accept the rule without question, demonstrating her faith and her good works as did Adam of old? Would not the Lord have blessed her for such obedience?

Mission rules exist to assist missionaries to achieve a high level of obedience, understanding, and love. The missionary who obeys the mission rules will someday bear grateful testimony of their divine help in his eternal progress and development.

Chapter 5

Faithfulness to the Lord

The apostle Paul reminds us that "it is required in stewards, that a man be found *faithful.*" (1 Corinthians 4:2; emphasis added.) If the question "Faithful to whom?" were posed, all would respond, "Faithful to the Lord!" It would never occur to the mind of any missionary to pledge allegiance or to show loyalty to a wicked and sinful purpose. Nevertheless, if there is any single recurring and grave problem in the mission field, it is expressly that.

For example, if a missionary commits some infraction of conduct, his companion, who is usually aware of the error, often fails to register righteous concern strongly enough to either stop the ill-conceived action or detain it long enough for assistance to arrive from his mission president or other mission leaders. By so doing the companion becomes faithful to the sin and the sinner and thus becomes a co-conspirator. The Lord has said:

> how oft you have . . . gone on in the persuasions of men.
> For, behold, *you should not have feared man* more than God. . . .
> *You should have been faithful.* (D&C 3:6, 7, 8; emphasis added.)

The key words pronounced in this passage denote a negative "You should not have feared man" and a positive "You should have been faithful."

Fear is the opposite of faith. The missionary who does not persuade his companion toward righteousness fails to do so, generally speaking, because of fear. He fears that his companion will become angry with him and that he will become the subject of his companion's and other missionaries' ridicule.

How many missionaries could have been saved from severance from the kingdom if the companion had said, "Elder, that is wrong! You know it, and I know it, so let's get back on track!" Most of the time a simple unwavering statement immediately issued forth at the suggestion of sin is sufficient to turn the direction of a misdirected companion. If the wayward missionary fails to yield, then the companion should relentlessly pursue to the point of seeking clarification of the issue from the district leader, the zone leader, or the president himself. If the issue has potentially grievous consequences, he should not fear to inform his president. In doing so he is faithful to his stewardship and is promoting righteousness. He is not to follow his companion into sin; rather, he is to lead him away from it. He must not wait until his companion is weeping the bitter tears of regret and facing the relentless weight of sinful actions, or he will come to the bitter realization that all might have been avoided if he had but been faithful to his charge and said no!

Too often when a proposed improper action meets with no resistance, it signifies a tacit agreement to join in. Agreeing to a seemingly harmless relaxation of the rules leads logically to additional rationalizations. Finally, that which never would have been considered in the beginning becomes accepted practice, leading to the bitter consequence of starting down the wrong path. It reaches out involvingly—taking in first one and then another, until little by little its web entangles not just one but many. That subtle process twists the intent of good missionaries and creates instead a totally distinct situation.

What happened to Elder Berry is a good example.

Elder Berry was an extraordinary missionary. He seemed to have a special ability to find, teach, and baptize the Lord's elect. By nature he was affirmative and endowed with what seemed to be an abundance of enthusiasm. Because of these gifts, he tended to give less credence to what he perceived to be the letter of the law. He openly expressed his view that mission rules were to help the missionary gain the ability to find, teach, and baptize. If that main objective was obtained, then the rest could be disregarded. He argued that, in effect, all of the rules were preparatory in nature and when the purpose was fulfilled, the rules could be appropriately disregarded. He reasoned that the rules must be superfluous for the "mature missionary" like himself.

To some, his logic seemed flawless. After all, Wilford Woodruff and other great missionaries of the past did not have today's mission rules, and they were successful. Soon others were convinced of the soundness of the proposition, and without a draft of constitution or bylaws there evolved a new organization—a small elite "club" within the mission for the "mature missionaries" only (those who had "superior wisdom and understanding"). It was heralded by its members as a step beyond the Lord's "normal" mission. It allowed special privileges to "superior" missionaries. They did not have to pay attention to the rules. They were above them.

Contrary to what had been originally intended by our gifted missionary, membership in the "elitist" group became dependent upon the missionary's willingness to attend an occasional movie, get up late, get out to work late, and so forth. Satan changed the rules to cater to the weak. He flattered their egos with thoughts of being superior while, in truth, their actions were inferior. He soothed their God-given conscience with the balm of false reasoning. They did not have the same responsibility to keep the "little mission rules," because the rules were to teach new missionaries the letter of the law until they too could live by the "spirit of the law."

Fortunately for that mission and for those missionaries, the mission president was brought to an awareness of this development by a faithful missionary, and a righteous path was soon reestablished. It is worthy of note that the majority of the missionaries involved in this episode were merely followers. They had followed as lambs to the slaughter so as not to create problems with their companions and with others. Unknown to them, their companions often had similar feelings, each thinking it was the desire of the other. All followed the group so as not to appear to be the dissenter. The tragedy of this case could have been avoided if one missionary had stood tall, took the Lord's affirmative, and unwaveringly decried the issue as false and dangerous.

A true leader is one who strides forward, signaling the correct road while all others appear to be eager to be misled. It is not so much a question of judgment. Virtually every missionary knows when he is doing wrong. Rather, it is a question of courage. Be a leader. Stand up and be counted should the occasion demand it. Be faithful to the Lord.

Faithfulness runs vertically from the missionary to our Heavenly Father. It does not run horizontally to a missionary's companion or to other missionaries. One cannot be faithful to the Lord and unfaithful to his companion at the same time. If a missionary does what the Lord would have him do, the companionship will always be assisted. There is nothing that can be classified as faithful to the Lord and damaging to the companion. But to be faithful to the desires of a wayward companion and totally unfaithful to the Lord is entirely possible.

Centuries ago Cain defensively responded to the Lord's inquiry regarding his brother Abel. "Am I my brother's keeper?" he asked. The Lord could have answered in the affirmative, "Yes, you are." Suppose a missionary went astray and the Lord were to ask his companion, "Missionary, where is thy companion?" and he received the response, "I don't know. Am I my companion's keeper?" Would the Lord be any more pleased with that reply than he was with Cain's?

A missionary *is* his companion's keeper. Each is to keep his companion safe from harm, be it physical, mental, spiritual, or emotional. If a missionary would not hesitate to physically pull his companion from dangerous oncoming traffic, then why would he hesitate to pull his companion to spiritual safety when oncoming temptations are about to crash into him? Is the soul of any less worth than the body? Does a missionary care less for the spiritual than the physical salvation of his companion?

Problems like this occur because the missionary has been conditioned to believe that acts of others are not his business. He lacks courage to take the first eventful step in assisting. The youth today are conditioned not to disclose incriminating information. They refer to it with negative expressions such as "ratting," "squealing," and "narking." They don't use more appropriate terms such as "keeper," "helper," or "being a loving and caring brother or sister." These terms are the ones which, in honesty, should be employed when a missionary saves his companion from the jaws of Satan by informing the mission president.

Logically, reconditioning the missionary's thinking is needed. Every newly called missionary should contemplate in advance what he would do if his companion were tempted to put his own salvation in jeopardy. To assist the missionary in this thinking, here are three proven guidelines which may appropriately be followed:

1. Have a firm attitude and an unwavering commitment to be faithful to the Lord.
2. Request clarification of the disputed rule from the district or zone leader.
3. Firmly indicate to the wayward companion that he should immediately speak with the mission president about the issue—or *you* will. Contemplated serious misbehavior or sin should never be left suspended. It must be taken care of at once.

Concerning this issue, President Spencer W. Kimball stated to a group of missionaries in South America in 1967:

> In one mission I came across a bad situation. One or two missionaries had been breaking the rules. All they did was go over to a certain home every Sunday night for dinner. The president didn't know anything about it. It wasn't perceived as anything very serious, but it was a regular occurrence every week. After a little while, these missionaries were bringing others to this home, and pretty soon they were doing a little flirting.
>
> The next thing we knew, there had to be an excommunication. I went there, and everything was revealed. I found that although there was only one boy who had actually gone to the extreme wherein he had to be excommunicated, there were about eighteen missionaries in the area who had followed like sheep over the ledge. They had not intended to do anything wrong. They had just followed the leadership. At first they had gone there only for meals, but then became engaged in little flirtations—not too deeply. But the thing is that there were eighteen missionaries who

knew that one had gone too far. They knew that he had been necking and petting, but not one of them would ever tell!

When I interviewed them, I asked, "Why didn't you tell the president that conditions were bad?" One of them said, "Well, that's none of my business! That elder can do as he pleases! If he wants to wreck his mission, that's okay with me. It's his business. It's his mission! If he wants to ruin his life, that's up to him. It's his life!"

And then I said to these elders, "Well, what about your missions? Isn't this your mission too? Isn't this your Church too? Are you willing to let one person do more damage than you can repair? Are you willing to have some missionary nullify all that you've done here? You've spent twenty months down here, elders, and you have been working reasonably hard, and at times you have done remarkably good work. Are you willing to permit that one scandal neutralize all that you've done—all of your efforts? That's what happens! Are you willing to do that?" He said, "Well, I hadn't thought of it like that."

Do you think that you have a loyalty? Where are your loyalties? Are you loyal to yourself? Are you loyal to your companion? Are you willing to let him go on and on and on, until he breaks his neck?

When he was excommunicated, it was a sad day in that mission because he was potentially a fine young man. All the missionaries loved him, and some of them were weeping that day. I remember! Some of them were weeping tears! Their brother was being excommunicated from the Church and sent home in disgrace!

And then I said to them, "Elders, do you know who excommunicated this boy? Not me. Not your president. Not the Elders' Court. It was you! You excommunicated your brother! How? Well, if you would have gone to this boy when you saw him breaking mission rules and said, 'Elder, let's not do that! That disrupts our whole program. We all lose spirituality when things like this happen.' "

Now suppose that he didn't yield and you said to him again, "Elder, you shouldn't do that! We can't be doing those kinds of things!"

And then suppose you'd gone a third time and said, "Elder, I'm sorry, but if you don't desist I'm going to have to report to the mission president, because I'm not going to let you destroy yourself! I think too much of you! I'm not going to let you destroy this mission! I think too much of it. I'm not going to let you destroy my work! I've worked too hard to have it all go to the wind! I'm going to tell the president, not as a tattle-tale, but I'm going to report to the president so that he can protect the whole program, if you don't desist!"

You see, there is nothing ugly about that, is there? That's the way it should be, because our loyalty is first to the Lord, then to the Church, the mission, and the world.

Logic, intelligence, and Spirit unite to give witness to our prophet's words. To do less than what he requests is to be a traitor to the sacred missionary call. Each ordained missionary should give heed and plan accordingly to be prepared to act in full accord with what the prophet has said. A companion's salvation could be at stake.

So think ahead, in case such a situation should ever face you. To be prepared is to be successful.

Chapter 6

Pure Motives

When the Lord first chastised Cain, he did so not because Cain had failed to offer up a sacrifice, but rather because his motives for offering the sacrifice were impure. Cain was following the counsel of Satan and not that of the Lord.

Today Satan offers counsel to the Lord's appointed ministers in the same way that he did to Cain. He does so in order to confuse them and render their efforts useless. If constant vigilance is not maintained, the end results can be disastrous. Such was the case of Elder Brown.

Elder Brown telephoned my home very late in the evening. He obviously was deeply troubled and wanted to see me. He had decided that he wanted to leave the mission and return home.

When he and his companion finally reached my home around midnight, he was behaving much like a caged animal. He paced back and forth across the room in an endless search for something he could not identify. He seemed almost possessed. After some preliminary talking to allow him some release of the tension he was feeling, we had prayer together. He then unfolded the events which had led him to my door in a fit of confused emotion.

Elder Brown was basically a fine missionary. He had searched the scriptures well in order to learn more about the power of faith. It was his desire to baptize converts. When he prayed, he prayed with fervor and zeal that he would be led to the doors of the Lord's elect.

That eventful night as he and his senior companion left their apartment he felt strongly impressed in a direct and powerful way to go to a certain home. His senior companion informed him that he did not have the same impressions but if it was his desire to go to that home, he would accompany him. As they went forth, Elder Brown, in an attempt to fortify his faith, repeated over and over in his mind, *I know this family will be waiting for us to arrive and will immediately ask for baptism.* He had heard of similar happenings. He felt that it was now going to be his opportunity for that experience. His desire carried him to an emotional state he had never before experienced. He was certain that a miracle was soon to be his.

When they arrived at the home, he rushed forward to knock. Time seemed endless. Why were the people not at the door ready to receive them? They knocked again and waited. They knocked a third and fourth time. It was his companion's voice that brought him to the cold reality of the situation.

"I guess they're not home, Elder," he said.

The next few moments were filled with confusion as Elder Brown tried relentlessly to reconstruct the feelings which had led them there. The harder he tried, the more confused he became. He had read of faith and of other missionaries being led to the doors of the honest in heart. He recalled his own promptings and how they had only led him to an empty house. Could it be that there was no such thing as faith? And if faith did not exist, then what about God? If God did not exist, then why was he on a mission? His mixed-up logic coupled with his internal feelings of confusion led him to his second major decision in one short evening. He decided that he should leave the mission field and go home. It was at that point that he telephoned me.

By the time he had reached the mission home he was in a complete jumble of confusion and was nearer to following the promptings of the adversary than those of his companion or the Spirit of truth. Finally, after fervent prayer the spirit of peace and tranquility joined us and we were able to reconstruct not only what had happened but more importantly why it had happened.

Why did Elder Brown receive the wrong feelings? What was it that led him to his erroneous conclusion? In retrospect the end result became obvious. Elder Brown desired to have a miracle. He wanted the Lord to tell him exactly where an elect family was waiting exclusively for him. Without realizing it, his motives had become more centered on his own glory and had become less and less pure. In his increasing desire to be the recipient of divine revelation, he had pushed into the background the main purpose for bringing souls to the Lord. His prominent, overriding desire was to receive—not to give.

The Lord could not respond to those impure motives, but Satan could. It was a simple matter for the adversary to suggest to his mind that a particular family was waiting just for him. In that moment he had, in effect, received his revelation. The elder jumped for the bait, thus adding more fuel to his misguided motive; and by the time he arrived at his destination, he had been completely deceived.

The next series of events was equally easy for Satan to promote. Frustration, confusion, and anger quickly developed into a climax of doubt. Elder Brown doubted prayer. He doubted faith. He even doubted his God for a moment. He certainly doubted his own divine calling as a representative of the Lord. Like Peter of old, Elder Brown saw the angry "waves" around him and started to sink in the "waters of despair." The design of the evil one was nearly complete. In fact, were it not for the Spirit's intervention, Elder Brown may have terminated his mission early, breaking the hearts of his parents and loved ones and failing to teach those who were waiting for him.

It is worthy of note that when Elder Brown announced to his senior companion his desire to visit a particular family, the response was negative. The companion flatly stated, "I do not have the same feelings." At this point it would have been appropriate for the senior companion to suggest prayer as the logical recourse to unite their feelings. He failed to do so, probably fearing that he might dispel his younger companion's enthusiasm for missionary work. Within his reach he had a marvelous opportunity to teach companionship prayer and its importance, the importance of companionship unity, pure motives, and correct principles of faith. But he failed to capitalize on the occasion.

Elder Brown did not notice that his motives were not entirely pure until the entire episode had happened. He was then able to view in retrospect how the adversary had tricked him. Since he did not clearly understand the law of having pure motives or the conditions contained therein, he was vulnerable. Had Elder Brown examined his own areas of weakness earlier, he could have effectively prepared himself against the onslaught. Clearly, it is essential to successful missionary work to understand that to have pure motives is to be pure in heart:

> The *pure in heart* are those who are free from moral defilement or guilt; who have bridled their passions, put off the natural man and become saints through the atonement (Mosiah 3:19); who have been born again, becoming the sons and daughters of Christ (Mosiah 5:17); who are walking in paths of uprightness and virtue and seeking to do all things that further the interests of the Lord's earthly kingdom. (*Mormon Doctrine*, p. 612.)

The Lord said, "Blessed are the pure in heart: for they shall see God." (Matthew 5:8.) He later indicated through Joseph Smith that most of the Saints could not yet be classed among the pure in heart (D&C 88:74). What better time and place is there to become pure in heart than the mission field? The steps to that goal are compatible with full-time missionary work. Missionaries must free themselves from moral defilement, or else they cannot serve. They must thrust aside the natural man through daily thought control and scripture study. Their paths must be straight. If they are to be successful, they must seek to do all things that would further the building up of the Lord's kingdom. The promise from the Lord to those who achieve these things is that they will be saved in his kingdom (D&C 124:54; 131:8). His holy invitation is extended to his ordained ministers of his gospel. The acceptance of his beckoning call to become totally pure in heart is to enter into those conditions which teach, train, and fortify one against Satan's attacks. It is a glorious opportunity which should not be lost. It requires only desire and effort. The Lord provides the rest.

Chapter 7

Personal Sacrifice

Missionaries sacrifice time, studies, money, careers, sports, talents, family, and friends for a specified amount of time for a higher calling—to teach the world that Jesus is the Christ, that his Church is restored, that Joseph Smith was his prophet, that the Book of Mormon is the Lord's witness, and that there is a living prophet today. When missionaries arrive in the field, additional personal sacrifices are required of them. Their living accommodations are usually inadequate. Often they have to learn a new language and adapt to a new environment as challenging cultures are thrust upon them. Those who travel to the far south or north may find that even the climates are changed. Such "sacrifices" are commonplace in the mission field.

Listing these numerous sacrifices may imply that the entire mission experience is destined to be a self-sacrificing, joyless existence. While a missionary may feel exactly this way some days, the consensus of virtually all missionaries is that these so-called sacrifices bring forth innumerable blessings. Even the most trying days are considered worthy material for personal diaries. Cold showers, boardinghouses with fleas, and beds without mattresses are all taken in stride as a higher object of devotion takes precedence.

The Lord has said: "And every one that hath forsaken houses, or brethren, or sisters, or father, or mother, or wife, or children, or lands, for my name's sake, shall receive an hundred-fold, and shall inherit everlasting life." (Matthew 19:29.)

To develop in them obedience, patience, and long-suffering, the Lord has required unusual personal sacrifices of some. The Prophet Joseph Smith spoke of his own tribulations in earnest supplication to his Father (D&C 121:1-7). Job's trials, Abraham's test, and President Spencer W. Kimball's physical afflictions are but a few additional examples.

The Lord gave us the supreme example at Gethsemane. Was that an easy task to accomplish? It was hard enough that the Lord cried out as he fell upon his face, praying, "O my Father, if it be possible, let this cup pass from me: nevertheless not as I will, but as thou wilt." (Matthew 26:39.)

In speaking of that great and last sacrifice, Amulek said: "For it shall not be a human sacrifice; but it must be an infinite and eternal sacrifice. Now there is not any man that can sacrifice his own blood which will atone for the sins of another." (Alma 34:10-11.)

That holy infinite sacrifice provoked immense suffering, "which suffering," reports the Lord, "caused myself, even God, the greatest of all, to tremble because of pain, and to bleed at every pore, and to suffer both body and spirit—and would that I might not drink the bitter cup, and shrink." (D&C 19:18.)

The suffering at Gethsemane required great sacrifice.

The suffering on the cross required great sacrifice.

The suffering at Liberty Jail required great sacrifice.

The persecution of the Saints in the early history of the Church represented great sacrifice on their part. How much sacrifice should be required of today's missionary? Is it too much of a sacrifice for him to get out of bed on time? Is it too much of a sacrifice for him to be out working on time? Is it too much of a sacrifice for him to be efficient in his day-to-day labors?

The Lord gave 100 percent in his atonement. Can missionaries give a 100 percent effort for two years of their lives?

President Ronald Loveland at a mission conference in Buenos Aires, Argentina, in January 1980, told of a missionary who had worked himself to utter exhaustion. When his companion tried to persuade him to go back to the apartment to rest, that he had done enough for one day, he said, "The Lord needs to know that I was serious when I said yes to my mission call." Was his sacrifice listened to from on high? It must have been. Today that missionary is a General Authority of the Church. The Lord knows that he is valiant.

The moving force for any missionary is his willingness to sacrifice a comfortable way of life to yield to a more holy purpose in order to effectively teach the gospel of Jesus Christ. Sacrifice of this nature brings forth blessings. Even though the level of sacrifice required generally of today's missionaries cannot be compared to that of old, it is still sacrifice. Today's missionaries sacrifice by daily doing those things which are difficult but important. Today's sacrifice requires consistent effort with an eye single to the glory of our Heavenly Father. Today's sacrifice requires a continual concern on the part of the missionaries to grow into perfection, an attitude that the status quo is unacceptable and an unquenchable desire to live the mission to its fullest.

Elder Victors came into the mission field unprepared. His pre-mission life was filled with mistakes and sadness. He had the wrong kinds of friends, the wrong motives, and the wrong habits. Before entering the mission field, he had failed to fully confess his sins. The only really good thing was that he had finally decided to change, and he was now willing to make the sacrifice to do so. The road back was not easy. He had much repenting to do, but he was determined to do it.

At first mission life was not easy. There were rules that were incompatible with his personal desires. What did he do? He sacrificed his desires. For example, prior to the mission he loved rock music. When he arrived in the mission field he sacrificed rock music for something better—talks with the Lord. He also was plagued with a physical problem. An old football back injury caused daily pain and sleepless nights. Month after month he sacrificed, gritted his teeth, and kept going.

Little by little his sacrifice started paying off. He made innocent mistakes, not completely understanding mission life, but some very special companions sacrificed some of their time to love and nurture him along until he could overcome his past. Soon he was made senior companion. Again there were some mistakes. With each mistake there was more personal sacrifice so that he did not make the same mistake again. He sacrificed his comfortable old way of life and replaced it with eternal values. Next he was made district leader. His district soared. He soon became the leading baptizer in the mission, not for a week or a month but month after month. His personal sacrifice was received by the Lord, and the Lord poured forth blessings abundantly. It was no surprise to anyone when Elder Victors was called to be assistant to the president. The single outstanding characteristic of Elder Victors's success was his understanding that personal sacrifice in doing the Lord's work brings forth blessings. He returned home from his mission a godlike man. The change was total. The principle of sacrifice was the changing agent.

There was another missionary who came into the field much better prepared and qualified than was Elder Victors. The difference was in his attitude relative to personal sacrifice. This elder was determined that he would not make any personal sacrifices during the mission. He would be a missionary, but he was not going to sacrifice anything. He liked his life-style and was determined that he would not change.

His mission was one of continued contention and misunderstanding. Because of his rebellious attitude he could not have the Spirit with him. And his rebellious attitude was a result of his determination to not sacrifice anything for his mission. He did not understand the law; therefore, the blessing pertaining to that law did not come forth. In spite of the fact that everyone tried to help him, he regressed. His personal commitment not to "change" had limited his progress. By the time he left the mission field he was notably less spiritual and more immature than when he had entered—all because he did not understand the law of personal sacrifice.

Missionaries are to eliminate their weaknesses by replacing them with strengths. Personal sacrifice to do that brings forth blessings. It is one of God's laws. Let it work for you.

SECTION 2

Principles of Proselyting

All successful missionary programs are founded upon sound principles of gospel-related truths. For example, President David O. McKay is credited with establishing among the members the principle "Every member a missionary." In truth, it was always intended for every member to be a missionary, but until President McKay coined the popular phrase its importance eluded most members. Yet while the principle was made popular by President McKay, by itself it meant very little in relation to bringing converts into the Church. Until specific programs were developed to express this divine principle, there was little direct membership increase in the Church. Clearly, unless divine truths are made part of a person's daily life, they are of little value to him.

The key to the development of mission or missionary programs rests in the missionary's ability to understand (find) the correct principle and then to build the proselyting techniques and programs upon that divinely inspired element. In order to bring better understanding of this concept, the following general categories are presented:

 1. The potential and power of missionaries.
 2. The power, dominion, and authority of faith.
 3. "Tracking" positives—a positive attitude in action.
 4. The way of the adversary.
 5. How to develop and maintain a successful mission.
 6. Members as finders of the Lord's elect.
 7. Missionaries as finders.
 8. Teaching, baptizing, and fellowshipping the Lord's elect.
 9. Guidelines for mission leaders.
10. The urgency of the work.

Chapter 8

The Potential and Power of Missionaries

Where did we come from? Why are we here? Where are we going? These standard questions are often asked of missionaries. The answers are to the point and are well known by members of the Church. In like manner the missionary might appropriately ask himself three similar questions. Who am I? What am I doing? How am I to do it?

The answers to these questions lead to an understanding of the divinity of the work and underscore its importance.

1. Who am I?

   Answer: I am a representative of the Lord Jesus Christ—a very sobering thought.

2. What am I doing?

   Answer: I am helping to roll forth the kingdom of God here on the earth as the other missionaries and myself cry repentance to every nation, kindred, tongue, and people.

3. How am I to do it?

   Answer: By following "every word that proceedeth out of the mouth" of our prophet.

> You are going out on your mission, not merely to make friends for the Church, though that is important, but to properly convert and baptize the numerous people who are anxious and ready for the gospel. Brethren, the spirit of our work must be urgency, and we must imbue our missionaries and Saints with the spirit of

"*now.*" We are not justified in waiting for the natural, slow growth which would come with natural and easy proselyting.

We believe that we must put our shoulder to the wheel, lengthen our stride, heighten our reach, increase our devotion so that we can do the work to which we have been assigned. (Message to new mission presidents by President Spencer W. Kimball as reported by Elder Bruce R. McConkie at a Mission Presidents Seminar on June 21, 1975.)

A Vision of Potential

Clearly, we have not yet realized our potential; were it so, we would not be challenged to "lengthen our stride, heighten our reach, and increase our devotion." To recognize our potential is to recognize the seed of divinity implanted within the soul of each of us. The accounts of great missionaries of the past describe the development of that seed within them. Wilford Woodruff was one of those great missionaries. He was baptized on December 31, 1833, and two days later he was ordained a teacher in the Aaronic Priesthood. Eleven months later he was sent on a mission. It was filled with difficulties and hardships—indifference to his message, persecution, hunger, exposure to the elements. When his companion decided to return home, he stayed, teamed up with another missionary, and went on to bring twenty people to baptism.

The divine seed continued to develop through missionary experience. In 1840, as an apostle, he was a missionary in England, still working on that potential. President Spencer W. Kimball comments:

> Wilford Woodruff, later to become president of the Church, went down from the Potteries and baptized a whole community numbering six hundred and more and about 60 ministers. He did not know it could not be done. He did not know that there was any limit. He did not know that two or three or four or five people, converts, was satisfactory. He only knew the word, "*all.*" (Message to new mission presidents at a Mission Presidents Seminar on June 21, 1975.)

There are missionaries who work far below their potential because they believe they have reached a level comparable with or close to that of other missionaries. They seem to have an automatic governor within their system which "controls" their work output. As soon as they compare favorably to others they immediately conclude they have reached their potential. They finish their missions and return home feeling satisfied. If they were to understand how far short they fell in reaching their potential, they would cry bitter tears. These missionaries are not necessarily lazy. They simply lack the vision of their true potential. President Kimball reminds us:

> I am told that a good golfer never plays against his opponent— he plays against par! A good runner runs against time—a good bowler works for 300—when they play against time, par, or a perfect 300, top performance is obtained through it. A mediocre game may be good enough to beat a poor opponent. The world is full of men who aimed only to be a little better than the other men of mediocrity. The history of the world is made by men who shoot for par and make it or better it. (Mission Presidents Seminar on June 21, 1975.)

The same phenomenon of not reaching one's potential also has occurred with an entire mission. For example, when a certain mission president began his labors, his mission was baptizing less than any of the surrounding missions. The missionaries resented being the lowest baptizers in the area. Little by little a sense of mission pride developed and they caught the vision, realizing that they could become the instruments in the Lord's hands to find and bring into his kingdom as many souls as the other missions. They worked diligently. They refused to give up, and the Lord saw their works and heard their prayers.

Some months later they reached their goal and even led all of the other missions. Then their automatic governor switched on, and they became satisfied to remain at that level. The Lord had poured out his blessings because of their faith and hard work. He did not suggest to them that they had reached their potential. *They* did that. They established their level of achievement according to what other missions had done. If they had heard that other missions were now finding and baptizing three or four times more, would they have been satisifed at their level? Of course not! They would have reasoned that more could be done, and they would have gone forth to meet the challenge set by the other missions.

Too often we establish our potential by looking at the achievements of others. Our gifts are not their gifts, and their level of attainment is not representative of our potential.

Reaching one's potential is dynamic. It requires a constant reaching out and up, a continual revision of goals. It requires a positive attitude. It requires spirituality. It requires faith—faith not so much in the missionary and his own capacity, but faith in the Lord that his potential is unlimited and that the missionary is merely a tool to be used.

In a Regional Representatives Seminar, President Spencer W. Kimball said:

> In Tempe, Arizona, in their university dairy they have found four cows that produce . . . 88,000 pounds of milk. That is 44 tons of milk, with 2,672 pounds, or over a ton of butter fat. They don't eat much more hay than any other cow—simply grain feed, careful management, careful milking, and proper feeding. . . . If cows can do it, people can do it! We can increase our production, and that is what we are talking about, and we want it to be real production, of course. We're not talking about baptisms—we're talking about conversions. (October 1975.)

Once the vision becomes clear, the missionary stops putting a ceiling on his potential and starts trusting in the Lord. He evaluates where he is. He decides where he is going. Then with all of his heart, might, mind, and strength he dedicates himself to achieving his goals. If he falls short, he identifies why and tries again. He is always trying, and he fights on in spite of the odds. He is continually adjusting and fine-tuning his plans to reach his potential.

Destination: Success

Much is said in the Church about the questions Where did we come from? Why are we here? and Where are we going? Aside from the religious connotation, each question has reference to purpose. Each carries with it the connotation that the Lord's divine undertaking is in operation. Man's destiny is not left to the whims of life. The Creator left nothing to chance. His eternal plan speaks of order, sequence of events, and activities which will test us. The plan refers to a specific timetable not given to man nor the angels but clearly established before the world was. Great blessings are promised to those who are valiant, and lesser blessings to those who are not. In every way, down to the last minute detail, the Lord set in motion his plan to reach his divine objectives: that man might be and that man might become like Him.

Are Goals Really Necessary?

Whether goals be divine or man-conceived, their importance cannot be shunned or put aside. Life goes on without man's goals, but predetermined direction does not. It is almost as difficult to reach an unknown destination as it is to return from a place one has never been to. Missionaries need to know their destination and how to arrive there. There is no time to waste in the mission field wandering to and fro without an objective clearly in mind. Missionaries need a target; without a target, they cannot plan. Without plans, they cannot succeed.

One author wrote that less than 3 percent of the people in the entire United States put their goals in writing. (Zig Zigler, *See You at the Top* [Gretna, La.: Pelican, 1974], p. 140.) Elder Thomas S. Monson once noted that a goal not written is only a wish. Think of it. More than 97 percent of the people in America are doing nothing more than wishing. What if the Lord had developed only 3 percent of the eternal plan, and the rest was merely a wish? Following that kind of planning, the world would not have been created, let alone function. If we are to become like the Lord, we must emulate his ways. We must *plan* to keep the commandments, not just *hope* to keep them. We must plan to be successful, not just hope to be successful. We must define our destination with accuracy and at the 100 percent level.

What Is a Goal?

At first glance this question may seem elementary. One might say, "A goal is a goal," "A goal is a state of intent," or

"A goal is what one wants to achieve." However, these statements still lack specificity.

For example, is the goal statement "I will not eat any food for twenty-four hours" a well-stated goal? If written with the intent to establish a twenty-four-hour fast, yes, it is acceptable. If the intent is to lose twenty-four pounds, however, the statement is not acceptable because it does not reflect the desired end results.

Webster's New Collegiate Dictionary defines *goal* as "the end to which a design tends." Often missionaries confuse the activity designed to reach the end result with the goal itself. "To work hard ten hours a day" is an example of the activity leading to the goal of "finding the Lord's elect." The goal to teach five discussions a day is only accurate if it is the desired end result. If the desired end result is to baptize a family a week, then the previous goal statements fall short of their mark. The first characteristic of a well-stated goal is that it accurately describes the desired end results. It is not to describe the activity which leads to its accomplishment.

Jean Henri Fabre, the great French naturalist, conducted an unusual experiment with some processionary caterpillars, so named because each follows the one in front of him. He arranged them in a circle on the rim of a flower pot so that the lead caterpillar was connected to the end caterpillar. They blindly started their march going around and around the flower pot. Seven days and nights they continued until finally they died of starvation (with food only inches away), all because they confused activity with accomplishment.

How to Set Goals

Goals are not for everyone. They serve a purpose only for those who want to succeed. J. C. Penney once said, "Give me a stock clerk with a goal, and I will give you a man who will make history. Give me a man without a goal, and I will give you a stock clerk."

Because all missionaries are meant to succeed, all missionaries must have goals. Their calling is divine—their purpose is eternal, and their message is sacred. There is far too much at stake for missionaries to fail. The question is not whether the missionary should set goals, but what kind he should set and how he should set them.

In addition to describing the desired end results, goals must have the following characteristics in order to be entirely meaningful and clear:

1. Goals should reflect a *specific quantity*. The goal statement "to baptize a lot of people" lacks specificity. "To baptize a family a week" is a much better goal statement.

2. Goals should be tied to a *specific time frame*. "I will find three new families before lunchtime" is definitive and communicates exactly what is proposed.

3. Goals should reflect a *specific quality*. "I will baptize three people by the end of the month who have music ability to help us develop the branch choir." The more specific the written goal, the clearer the work guideline for the missionaries.

4. Goals should be challenging but *realistic*. Past performance and future potential are the chief considerations in setting realistic but challenging goals. For example, the goal of fifty baptisms for the month of March is not realistic if the missionary has never baptized more than two in a month—unless, of course, the potential of the area has changed drastically.

5. Goals should be *set daily*. A monthly baptismal goal is too broad to serve the missionary well. It only begins to be of service as it is broken down into weekly and then daily, short-range goals. The missionary must pay attention to all of the daily activities which promote the attaining of the goal, but he should be careful not to confuse those daily activities with the goal itself. The accomplishment of goals through daily dedication and discipline is one of the best builders of character that missionaries have.

As the missionary sets his own goals, he can easily review these five characteristics of well-written goals to check the quality of his own goal statement. Goals which describe the desired end results with the specific characteristics listed above are well-written goals.

The power of the sun shining through a powerful magnifying glass will never start a fire if the glass is moved all around. Once the sun's rays are concentrated in one place, their energy is focused on a specific target and things get hot. Daily goals help the missionary to focus on the target. The smart hunter does not shoot the covey, he selects one quail as a specific target. Missionaries should zero in on their target and set daily goals.

Once missionaries learn to evaluate the exact amount of time and effort it takes to accomplish a specific goal, they often extend that training into their goals concerning personal development. Elder Gregory was an outstanding example of this. He loved to study the scriptures. His problem was time. Managing his district leadership responsibilities, maintaining a high level of successful proselyting work, and being a model senior companion seemed to absorb "all" of his time. It seemed impossible to find an extra hour each day to read more than what could be read during the time allotted for gospel study.

He would not give up. He timed himself and found that it took him only fifty seconds to read a page in the Book of Mormon. He reasoned that he could probably find several fifty-second periods each day if he always had his Book of Mormon with him to take advantage of that time. Instead of trying to find a quiet hour of undisturbed time, he looked for any available spare moment. He found that in spite of his hectic schedule there were many occasions when he could read several pages, such as when he was traveling in the car to district meetings or to other appointments. As he stirred hot cereal on the stove, he could read a few additional pages. Soon he was reading a minimum of thirty pages and sometimes as high as fifty pages per day—all during the time that he "did not have."

Because he enjoyed reading the scriptures and because it was his own personal goal, he did not mind the sacrifice of taking a quick shower instead of the long one that he had enjoyed so much. His desire was to read the Book of Mormon. He had calculated that if he could read thirty pages a day as a matter of habit, he could completely read the Book of Mormon in seventeen and a half days. If he maintained that pace, he could read the Book of Mormon thirty-seven times during his mission (in addition to his regular scripture study). All of this could be done with the time that he "did not have."

A miracle? Perhaps so. Miracles often take place when missionaries are that dedicated and are correctly taught how to set goals. They have to know the consequences of their decisions and be realistic in their goals. They must have determination and dedication to their goals in order to turn goals into reality. This is the final indicator of success.

Chapter 9

The Power, Dominion, and Authority of Faith

The apostle Paul defined faith as "the substance of things hoped for, the evidence of things not seen." (Hebrews 11:1.) The Prophet Joseph Smith amplified Paul's affirmation by noting that "Faith is . . . the moving cause of action in . . . intelligent beings." He explained that it is the first great governing principle which has power, dominion, and authority over all things. (*Lectures on Faith*, 1:7-8.)

It is common for missionaries to want the "power, dominion, and authority" spoken of by the Prophet so that their investigators may be converted. Missionaries have often said that they "know" that a particular family is going to be baptized. They go forth in a spirit of positive attitude "knowing" this or that family will enter into that holy covenant. Unfortunately, not all of these "known" families reach the waters of baptism. Some fall away. Christ noted in his parable of the sower that the devil "cometh . . . and taketh away the word out of their hearts, lest they should believe and be saved." (Luke 8:12.)

If a missionary repeats in his mind and to others, "I know that the Jones family will be baptized, I know that the Jones family will be baptized," what happens to this missionary if the Jones family is not baptized? The missionary may continue zealously trying to promote a higher degree of faith with the same affirmative words for every family, only to find his faith diminishing with his repetitious phrases. He needs to clearly understand that every investigator has been guaranteed the fundamental right of free agency. God must obey his own laws. Since man has free agency, God may force no man to heaven.

> Know this, that every soul is free
> To choose his life and what he'll be,
> For this eternal truth is given
> That God will force no man to heav'n.
> ("Know This, That Every Soul Is Free," *Hymns,* no. 90.)

The missionary who tries to build faith by using only a positive attitude does not understand how true faith is increased.

> *Faith is a gift of God bestowed as a reward for personal righteousness.* It is always given when righteousness is present, and the greater the measure of obedience to God's laws the greater will be the endowment of faith. (*Mormon Doctrine,* p. 264.)

Thus we see that the fundamental ingredient of faith is personal righteousness. If one is worthy, true faith can be increased regardless of an expression of positive thinking or a lack thereof.

A positive attitude should be an expression of knowledge and a product of faith. Faith and knowledge are not products of positive attitude. There is great power in maintaining a positive attitude (see chapter 10), but it should not be confused with the power of faith.

> *Faith is based on truth and is preceded by knowledge. Until a person gains a knowledge of the truth he can have no faith.* (*Mormon Doctrine,* p. 262.)

If the missionary has no knowledge, i.e., "inspiration or revelation," then he is exercising only the power of a positive attitude when he boldly proclaims that a particular family will be baptized. On the other hand, if the Holy Spirit has whispered to his soul that this family will be baptized, then he is merely confirming that of which he has been divinely informed.

The sequence is always the same. To have faith, one must be righteous. The righteous receive the power of faith as a gift. The greater the measure of obedience to God's laws, the greater will be the endowment of faith and power.

Miracles, signs, the gifts of the Spirit, the knowledge of God and godliness and every conceivable good thing—all these are the *effects of faith. (Mormon Doctrine, p. 264.)*

If he clearly understands that faith depends upon his righteousness, then the obedient missionary has claim to added faith and power. One of the most valuable gifts or products of faith in missionary work is the power of discernment. If all missionaries were able by the power of the Spirit to identify those among the masses of people who are "on the Lord's side," then the building up of the kingdom would accelerate dramatically.

The key to finding the Lord's elect is to be totally worthy. Worthy missionaries often report special blessings (i.e., that they were not responsible for finding investigators; rather, the investigators found them).

For example, Elder Tidwell and his companion were inspired to leave their boardinghouse during a torrential rainstorm to travel, soaking wet, on their bicycles to an unknown destination. While traveling they were stopped by the driver of a pickup truck —a stranger who had also left his own apartment in the rain for "unknown" reasons. This man stopped the missionaries and asked them how he could acquire a copy of the Book of Mormon. He was baptized a short time later.

Elders Gardner and Powell report their own experience: "One day my companion and I were walking through a shopping area, trying to think of a good way to talk to the people there about the gospel. All of a sudden a man selling fruit threw us each an apple. He called out his address and asked us to come by. We didn't say a word the whole time. We thought it was some kind of a joke. We later went by his home and have now taught this family of four the gospel of Jesus Christ and challenged them for baptism. They said yes." (Argentina Buenos Aires North Mission, 1980.)

These gifts from on high are bestowed upon the righteous. They come with power, dominion, and authority. Each missionary needs to strive diligently to increase his power of faith through righteous living, that he may reach his divine potential.

Chapter 10

"Tracking" Positives—A Positive Attitude in Action

Mission life is challenged daily by those who think differently, act differently, are motivated differently, and have different values, desires, aspirations, and intentions. The missionary needs to constantly seek the qualities of unity, harmony, and love. Unless he understands basic principles of how such might be accomplished, he is left to the frustration and often contention of each issue. If through his own action he can influence the behavior of others and instill unity, harmony, and love in those with whom he works, he greatly increases his effectiveness as a missionary (not to mention increasing his own happiness).

Changing Someone's Behavior

Basically there are three ways to change the behavior of another. The first consists in carefully following the behavior of the selected person, and the moment he does something contrary to that which is desired, punishing him in some fashion so that he might learn that his actions are unacceptable. Parents often follow this pattern with their children—exercising punishment which ranges from verbal reprimand—"Don't put your feet on the chair!" "Don't slurp your food!" "Don't talk back!"—to actual physical punishment.

The second way to change behavior is to reinforce that behavior which is acceptable and ignore that which is unacceptable. A parent praising a child for his accomplishments is representative of this. For example: "Son, you received an *A* in your history class. I'm proud of you!" "Thank you very much for clearing the table for your mother, Mary. That was very thoughtful of you."

The third form of changing behavior is a combination of these two patterns. When the child does something not acceptable, he is told so; and when he does something compatible with the desired behavior, he is also told so.

The Lord gave a more exact formula when he said:

> No power or influence can or ought to be maintained by virtue of the priesthood, only by persuasion, by long-suffering, by gentleness and meekness, and by love unfeigned;
>
> By kindness, and pure knowledge, which shall greatly enlarge the soul without hypocrisy, and without guile—
>
> Reproving betimes with sharpness, when moved upon by the Holy Ghost, and then showing forth afterwards an increase of love toward him whom thou hast reproved, lest he esteem thee to be his enemy. (D&C 121:41-43.)

Note carefully the words the Lord selected to teach this principle: 1) persuasion, 2) long-suffering, 3) gentleness, 4) meekness, 5) love unfeigned, 6) kindness, 7) with pure knowledge, 8) without hypocrisy, 9) without guile. He limited negative action to reproving with sharpness, which was to be done only when the Holy Ghost prompted it; and then the one reproving was to show forth an increased love toward the one reproved.

Think of the last time you had occasion to reprimand someone. Did you do so because the Holy Ghost moved you to? Did you hear a whispering to your soul telling you that, out of love and concern for your brother, you should reprove him? Or did you reprimand him because you were angry? The last time you had an argument with someone, did you do so because the Holy Ghost told you to contend with your brother, or did you do so because contention arose from some other source? The Lord has said, "he that hath the spirit of contention is not of me." (3 Nephi 11:29.) He counsels to "let no man strive, nor reprove another." (Hosea 4:4.) In a word, any reproach should be initiated only when so directed by the Spirit.

"Tracking" Positives

Out of the three methods previously stated, "tracking positives," or reinforcing positive behavior and ignoring the negative, is the fastest way to change someone's behavior. This concept became very clear to me some years ago when I was a member of a consulting team contracted to assist in the training of personnel in a large well-known company in Chicago, Illinois. During the few days we were there it became obvious that there was a great deal of dissatisfaction with one of the receptionists. It was obvious why everyone unanimously wanted her services terminated. She was lazy and belligerent and lacking in skills, capacity, and tact. It seemed as if she went out of her way to cause problems.

The company was particularly concerned because this secretary represented the management's first attempt to employ unqualified people from minority groups and to help them develop their skills and talents through inservice training. One of the tasks given to us was to help that young lady become a competent secretary. Some jokingly referred to the project as "Mission Impossible."

One day this secretary, whom we will call Mary, received a telephone message for one of the salesmen. It was not uncommon for her to pay little attention to such messages, but on this occasion she did note the telephone number of the calling client. She did not write down the name of the salesman for whom the message was taken, however, nor the company that the client represented. Even the date was forgotten. The telephone message was not given to the salesman but was carelessly cast aside to finally end up trampled on the floor. It was only by accident that the salesman noticed it as he was passing by Mary's desk.

Picking it up, he recognized the telephone number of his most important client and immediately telephoned to see if he could be of service. Imagine his surprise to find out that the company had decided to upgrade all of the computer equipment in their large plant; and because the salesman had not returned their call, they assumed that he was not interested and had therefore made the decision to buy from a competitor.

The salesman tried desperately to assure the company that he was indeed interested. He insisted that if they would but give him time, he would do, free of charge, a complete needs analysis for their projected equipment upgrade. Finally, after much persuasion the company agreed to give him time to assess their future needs and submit a proposal. After many days of nearly round-the-clock work, the salesman was successful. His proposal was accepted by the company, and he was rewarded with a handsome bonus from his own company for his hard work.

It was at this point that he came to us. He insisted that Mary be discharged. Her sloppy work habits had nearly cost him his largest account, he argued. Not only had she neglected all of the pertinent information on the telephone message, but more importantly had failed to give it to him at all. Had he not noticed it on the floor, he would surely have lost his best and largest client. He maintained that her attitude was not only a detriment to him but to the whole company. He was determined that she be fired.

We asked him to try one last experiment with us. We explained to him the importance of helping her to change her attitude and the process of reinforcing positive actions and ignoring negative ones. We reviewed step by step everything that had occurred. The only positive act that we could identify was that she had, in fact, taken the telephone message. Clearly, the message as taken was not as complete as we would have desired, and she did not follow through. But after all, she had taken the message, and we had to identify a positive act.

We now asked the salesman to go to the nearest florist and buy her some flowers. He rebelled. He was not going to give her a gift for having nearly lost for him his most important client. We prevailed, and finally he did as requested.

He returned from the florist with a single long-stem rose in an attractive, small white vase. He presented it to her with a note that read: "To Mary, Because you took the time to record that particular message, I was able to make a large sale. Thank you. Bill."

What effect did this little act of kindness have upon Mary? All of a sudden she started taking down every telephone message that came in. She made certain that each was received by the appropriate salesman. Clearly, she enjoyed being rewarded with kindness. Her belligerent attitude was a defense mechanism to cover up her fear of failing. The salesmen, in turn, recognized the change in her attitude and responded accordingly. When she did something right, they complimented her on her work. Her supervisor pointed out to her that the letter she had typed last week had fourteen errors but that her latest letter had only seven. He noted that if she continued to progress at that rate, he would have no other option but to request a pay increase for her.

Mary started to have a better self-image. Her dress and general attitude improved as if overnight. And it all occurred because someone ignored all of the negative aspects and focused only on her positive qualities. In the beginning all had agreed that there were no positive aspects about her at all. As she progressed, it was as if everyone was pulling for her to succeed. Everyone took joy in her progress. Everyone participated in her advancement.

Some few years later I was in New York City on business. While there I decided to call upon my old friend who was the director of the training center wherein I had been a consultant. He had now risen to the rank of executive vice-president of that large and important company. I was directed from floor to floor until I finally arrived at the top floor of the skyscraper. I found myself in a roomy, very expensively decorated executive suite.

Soon a very attractive young lady came to personally accompany me into the inner office of my successful friend. He greeted me with affection. Then turning to his executive secretary, he said, "You remember Mary, don't you?" I could hardly believe my eyes. Could this attractive young lady possibly be the same girl who, a few short years earlier, was the least likely to succeed? She laughed warmly and said, "I wondered if you would remember me." It was indeed the same young woman. She was immaculately dressed, and self-assurance emanated from her very being. She fitted well into the corporate environment. She ob-

viously was well respected. Her poise and good manners were
exemplary. My friend later told me that he had never had such
an outstanding and competent executive secretary. In every
aspect she was superior.

The Lord rarely calls any of us for what we are, but rather
for what we can become. The same environment of love and
support which caused Mary to grow can do the same for you and
others. The capacity and potential is there. It only needs development, as the Lord stated, by persuasion, long-suffering, gentleness, meekness, love unfeigned, kindness, and pure knowledge,
without hypocrisy and without guile. These are the ingredients
of successful interpersonal relations. Positive response to appropriate behavior brings forth positive results. Love begets love. It
is a law. Bringing to light negative behavior by magnifying it also
provokes negative results unless: 1) reproving with sharpness is
done only when moved upon by the Holy Ghost, and 2) the one
reproving shows forth afterwards an *increased* love, "lest he
esteem thee to be his enemy."

Let's examine how this concept may function in the mission
field.

A certain lady missionary seemed to have trouble with every
companion she had. She had an ability to analyze every situation. She could identify why someone was motivated to act in a
given way. Each time there was a conflict, she was able to ratio-
nally and logically understand the dynamics of the situation and
be relatively unmoved emotionally—truly a great gift and talent.
With her understanding of each issue of contention, she would
unhesitatingly describe and unfold the events to her companion,
noting wherein the companion had failed and what she should
have done. The net results were always the same. Unable to
understand emotionally, her companions were reduced to tears.
They perceived her as an enemy because she seemed to lack
understanding and compassion.

I attempted on one occasion to explain to her the process of
tracking positives. She responded with the usual demonstration
of her ability to analyze what was going on. She explained that
she was aware of the direction in which the conversation was
heading and the intent of it, and she then explained again to me

wherein her companion had failed. She was so intent upon demonstrating her superior abilities that she had become, for the time being, unteachable.

It was only after suffering through several more companionship trials that she again arrived at my office—this time prepared to openly explore the possibility of improving her own involvement in the companionship. Since she was clearly able to discern the motivation of her companions, I suggested that she start tracking those actions which would positively reinforce the desired behavior. Simply stated, she "rewarded" her companion for the good things she did and ignored all of the bad. A gift of a little flower here, a thank-you note there, and the miracle took place. In a matter of just a few days they were enjoying each other. Two weeks later they loved each other. Just as importantly, the work went forward with much more success. Soon their relationship was well established and harmony was achieved.

In order to achieve a harmonious relationship, it is helpful to try to identify the true motivation behind a negative behavior. For example, Elders Higgins and Worth were perplexed. The bishop of the ward where they were assigned was seemingly opposed to missionary work. Everything the elders wanted to do was openly opposed. Special missionary activities were discouraged or not calendared by the bishop. In fact, the bishop went out of his way to criticize the missionaries' efforts and to discourage baptisms in his ward. He even attempted to intervene in the candidate's baptismal interview for worthiness.

The two missionaries had received training relative to changing a negative attitude, but they had never had occasion to put it into practice. Obviously this was their golden opportunity. Instead of criticizing the bishop's actions, they tried to identify the reason why he was being so negative. It did not take much research to have some issues come to light. First, the bishop's ward had the highest inactivity rate of any ward in the stake. Second, his home teaching program was not functioning. Any new members added to his rolls made the home teaching problem even worse. He did not have enough home teachers as it was, let alone additional teachers to visit the newly baptized and to present them the Church-prescribed lessons. Third, the stake president was his relative. He certainly did not want to appear to be a failure in the eyes of his family; therefore, he reasoned that he must slow down the proselyting program of his ward—at least until he could stimulate an improved home teaching program.

Once the missionaries determined the bishop's probable motivation, they took steps to assist him in solving some of his problems. They identified all the people who had been baptized in the ward for the last year. They worked out a plan of reactivation for those who had fallen into inactivity, which included programs to train the newly baptized to be effective home teachers. They reasoned that the bishop's problem was also their problem. Unless the ward was better prepared to absorb new members, many more converts would fall into inactivity.

After the missionaries had carefully analyzed the problem and had worked out their detailed plans, they requested time to meet with the bishopric. Time was granted. Imagine the bishop's surprise when the two missionaries showed a supportive attitude and unfolded a plan to resolve the bishop's major problem. The bishopric accepted the missionaries' proposal almost without modification, and the program was launched.

Within the week the reactivation program started to work. True to their word, the missionaries reactivated family after family. As they did so, they divided with the home teachers and trained the local brethren to give the lessons prescribed for new members. Within a month there was a new excitement within the ward. The reactivated members returned with enthusiasm. The young bishop sensed the change and responded accordingly.

Can you imagine the mission president's pride in those two missionaries? They had the maturity to respond not as they were being responded to but rather with persuasion, long-suffering, gentleness, meekness, love unfeigned, kindness, pure knowledge, and without hypocrisy or guile; they accepted their challenge and productively changed not only the attitude of the bishop but that of the whole ward. Tracking positive attitudes, looking for reasons behind any negative behavior, and solving the problem was their simple motto; and it worked.

The Power of a Positive Attitude

There exists in the Church a mission that is considered "hard" by most of those who were called to serve there. All of the statistical reports of that mission confirm those judgments. As new missionaries arrive, they are informed by the others that "this mission is not a high baptizing mission." When the new missionary hears such utterances, he almost always accepts it automatically, without question, and the mission continues on at the established level of low performance.

Elder Michaels arrived in that mission. Prior to his call he had often gone out with the full-time missionaries. He knew their programs and knew their trials, but most of all he knew their attitude. Those missionaries had a positive frame of mind. If they came up against an obstacle, they used it as a stepping-stone. There was an entirely different prevailing attitude in his home mission.

As Elder Michaels listened to the negative expressions of his new companions, he resolved that he would not allow them to affect his efforts. Until he found out on his own that the mission was indeed "impossible," as it was often referred to, he would not give in.

He found himself alone. His senior companion was soon to go home and was one of the head protagonists in keeping up the negative image of the mission. "The mission is hard," he proclaimed; therefore, "there's little use in trying." He went through the motions but did little else.

Elder Michaels was frustrated by his companion's attitude, but he did not give in to the insistent propaganda. His positive attitude remained intact. Soon he was the companion to a relatively new missionary who had not been totally conditioned into believing that the mission was impossible. They decided they would take the responsibility upon themselves to change the attitude of the mission by proving the other missionaries wrong. They knew that the Lord could use them to find, teach, and baptize his people and were determined to do so.

The hours were long and their bodies tired, but little by little they were able to build a pool of investigators. Then the baptisms began. These missionaries knew that for the Lord nothing is impossible. They trusted in him and in his power.

As families were baptized, these new members became interested in sharing the gospel with their friends and relatives. The Lord again poured forth his blessings. At first the missionaries were baptizing once every three months. Soon they were baptizing every month, and finally, they were baptizing nearly every week. At one point Elder Michaels and his companion were baptizing nearly one-third of all of the converts in the entire mission.

Hard mission? Mission Impossible? Or only the results of a negative attitude?

Missionaries should have faith that the Lord will bless them if they are righteous. They should have faith that there is nothing impossible for the Lord. They should go forth with the power of their convictions expressed in action and in a positive attitude—that is the driving force that will persuade men and women to repent and be baptized. The missionary who, with a positive attitude, cries out for all to hear, "I know that the Lord lives; I know Joseph Smith was a prophet; I know the Book of Mormon to be the word of God; I know that you can know it too"—that missionary will be blessed beyond measure.

Chapter 11

The Way of the Adversary

It takes very little time for a missionary to realize that the mission field is similar to a battlefield. As soon as his call is received, temptations come to the missionary as "flies to a carcass." The missionary becomes the prime target of the adversary. If Satan can cause a missionary to fail in his divine task, those who were waiting for his message of truth are at best left to continue their wait for others. Satan knows that the conversion of a young married couple today results in twenty to forty souls embracing the gospel within two generations. To conquer one missionary is to thwart the progress of many.

Those who are called to serve must thrust in their sickles with all their might, take full advantage of the gospel tide, and take care not to fall into the tempter's snares.

Experienced missionaries become more wary as success increases. Mission success provokes reaction from the one who is disturbed by increased conversions. If the missionary cannot be stopped, the investigator becomes the center of the attack. The Lord warns of this in the parable of the sower:

> Now the parable is this: The seed is the word of God.
> Those by the way side are they that hear; *then cometh the devil, and taketh away the word out of their hearts,* lest they should believe and be saved. (Luke 8:11-12; emphasis added.)

Every missionary would do well in reviewing this scripture, or others like it, after every discussion with those who feel the spirit of the word of God.

The adversary will not allow conversions to take place without trying to intervene with his evil forces. Investigators should be told that ill-informed relatives, friends, and others may come to them with statements regarding the Church. They should invite the bearers of such tidings to meet with the missionaries and investigate open-mindedly the teachings of salvation.

Missionaries should inform the investigators that such an attack can be a sign to them, and they may discern the fountain of such misconceptions by being forewarned. Their literal salvation rests completely upon the missionaries' preventing the word of God from being taken from them. Missionaries must turn the investigators' attention to the word of God and teach them not to trust in "the arm of flesh" for the truth. It is important to reiterate to them the Lord's promise that "By the power of the Holy Ghost ye may know the truth of all things." (Moroni 10:5.)

The adversary will attack the investigator, his friends, and, of course, the missionaries. Also, when a mission is progressing, it is common for the entire mission to feel the influence of the evil one. The situation detailed below demonstrates how his battle plan may shift.

President White had carefully watched the progress of the mission. Each month seemed to be a repetition of the previous month. The mission was progressing well. Baptisms had more than doubled over the previous year. The president interviewed every missionary in his geographically small mission every four weeks and had zone and multi-zone conferences often in an attempt to keep the missionaries informed as to potential pitfalls and to be on top of any problems. The missionaries seemed to pull together, and their moral and spiritual level was at an all-time high.

Month after month the attack of the adversary was directed against the mission as a whole. Any deviation from this pattern had been readily identifiable by the mission president in interview sessions and zone conferences. Then the adversary's tactics changed. Instead of a general attack, key individual missionaries were selected, as the battle shifted to a divide-and-conquer tactic. A district leader, one of four elders living together, was subtly distracted in such a cunning way that it wasn't until later that he recognized how he had been led astray. It happened so slowly that at first it was only a game. He jokingly included the other three missionaries in the "fun" of the occasion. They too joined in with careless gaiety. As soon as all were involved, temptations grew in proportion.

Shortly, all of these elders were breaking additional mission rules and the Spirit had left them. Because of their deep involvement and their feelings of guilt, they were reluctant to inform their mission president of the transgressions. Because the issue was isolated from the rest of the mission, it was not evidenced in the zone conferences or the interviews. By the time it finally came to light, the entire district was in spiritual darkness.

At the same time, similar problems were taking place in several other areas within the mission. The shift in the tactics of the adversary was sufficient to hide the new attack from the mission president's view.

As the president interviewed each wayward missionary, a precious truth was revealed. In each case, the missionary had been tempted at his weakest point. Satan did not tempt the Savior with food when he was filled and satisfied. He waited until the Lord was weak from fasting, and then he launched forth a specific temptation for a specific "weakness." All of us are viewed in a similar fashion. We are known by Satan and his host of followers. We lived together with them in a premortal state, and since those spirits who, like us, would become embodied outnumbered them there by only about two to one, it seems probable that some of them are well acquainted with us. No doubt they watch our progress here on this earth. They know our mortal weaknesses. They have been here to see each fallacy take place as the snares were prepared. With each departure we make from the truth, we relinquish to them more power over us. Little by little we cross further over into the enemy's territory.

Given their knowledge of us and our weaknesses, it seems only logical that we must take evasive action lest we be snared and our souls destroyed. It is not enough merely to be aware of the present battle plan of the adversary. The Saints of the Most High also need to aggressively attack current evil tactics and not just defend themselves against those tactics. Our attack is not to be directed against the adversary, however, but against our own weaknesses. Every missionary knows himself better than anyone else does. He knows his weaknesses, and he knows his strengths. The battle is either to eliminate his weaknesses one by one or to make them his strengths. If he does this, Satan will have lost his advantage.

For example, when President White became aware of the tactics of the evil one, he adopted both a defensive and an offensive attitude. He first made everyone aware of the shift in direction of the attack and then initiated the mission "sacrifice" program. In that program each missionary was encouraged to progressively sacrifice specific weaknesses that made him vulnerable to Satan's advances or to build the weaknesses into strengths. Personal progress was initiated and soon mission progress was noted. Those who were diligent in this righteous endeavor were exceedingly blessed. Those who sacrificed less continued to live in a dangerous zone. They were still vulnerable and remained the targets of the adversary.

A missionary's protection is to build his own fortification and to develop his own state of perfection. The Lord's admonition is clear: "Be ye therefore perfect, even as your Father which is in heaven is perfect." (Matthew 5:48.) In the instance discussed, the mission program to eliminate personal weaknesses was successful, and it was used throughout the mission to promote each missionary's personal growth and protection.

We can readily draw examples from this program. The missionary who replaces a quick temper with patience is blessed. The missionary who sacrifices occasional gossip for positive comments is blessed. The more a missionary builds his defenses against the potential attacks of the adversary, the more he is blessed.

The steps for such personal progression are not complicated. They consist of:

1. Identification of the character trait which is undesirable or weak.

2. Selection of the character trait which will replace the old undesirable trait.
3. Development of a self-improvement program which eliminates or modifies the undesirable trait and leads one toward the desirable trait.

Elder Redcliff, a Blackfoot Indian from the reservations of Montana, was shy. He wanted to be a bold missionary but did not know how to overcome his shyness. He developed his "program" to overcome his fear of speaking up. He decided he would tackle the problem in stages.

He began by greeting people in a strong voice. (He did this by imagining they were three to four yards further away from him than they really were, which meant he had to raise his voice to the level that others normally used. He decided to do this until he was able to do it without fear.

His next step was to make without hesitation a statement of fact to an investigator or contact. In order to do so, he studied with extra diligence before meeting with a particular person or family. His statement was carefully planned and he was prepared for its delivery. Since he knew his subject well, his self-confidence grew in leaps and bounds.

The final step of his program was to deliver an entire missionary discussion in a firm, loud (loud to him) voice with conviction and boldness.

After diligent endeavor, he achieved his goal. He was full of pride and satisfaction, because he had built his weakest character trait into a tower of strength.

Since Satan attacks the weak areas of our character, each wise missionary will methodically and systematically identify his own weaknesses, build programs of defense, and little by little overcome "the flesh" by putting on the armor of God. In so doing he initiates his own continual plan of "sacrifice," progressing toward finite perfection (the proper foundation for the development of infinite perfection or godhood). In so doing, he also protects himself from the tempter's snare. The point of emphasis is that now is the time for missionaries to initiate a program of self-sacrifice and improvement.

Missionaries have a unique opportunity for personal and

spiritual preparation under conditions which greatly favor growth and development and offer a strong foundation for future life. For example, the missionary who is used by the Lord feels his Spirit often and grows spiritually from each experience. A variety of additional spiritual manifestations takes place as the lives of men and women he influences are molded to fit gospel principles. Miracles take place. Alcoholics leave their liquor. Smokers abstain. Adulterers and fornicators abruptly and completely change their lives. The gifts of tongues, discernment, and healing, and the power of the holy priesthood of God also are manifested in the course of normal missionary work.

During this limited but spiritually provocative time the wise missionary takes advantage of these blessings and prudently prepares his character, building it up so Satan's temptations will not later weaken him. Because of such shelter, he can grow and flourish spiritually, perhaps as in no other time of his life. The mission is indeed the perfect time to fortify against Satan's attacks and to establish through thought control and self-discipline a firm spiritual foundation for life. Therein exists the divine law, and therein exists the divine blessings.

Chapter 12

How to Develop and Maintain a Successful Mission

Perfection in missionary programs and procedures does not yet exist. There is still adequate room for improvement regardless of what is currently being done. The key is to identify the day-by-day missionary activities that are a part of the entire mission process. Once identified, they can be carefully analyzed and evaluated by addressing the following kinds of questions: How does one plan and organize in order to accomplish each task? What tools are necessary? Can an inexperienced missionary do it? How does one start? How can the process be improved upon? Is it bringing about the desired results? Is there a better way to do it?

Carefully analyzing each procedure by following it through a series of these kinds of questions will bring one to the logical conclusion of improving the way missionary work is being done, thus developing the mission into a more successful one. To illustrate this concept, I refer to an incident which, although it does not relate to missionary work, does portray the basic principle that whatever is being done at the present time can be improved. It is the application of this principle that leads to developing a more successful mission.

Some years ago a few selected graduate students from a midwestern university were sent to local companies to test their abilities in analyzing administrative procedures. They were to make recommendations to their professor of changes they would make if they were the president of the company to which they were assigned.

One student was assigned to visit a large local hospital. He was to select an administrative procedure and attempt to improve it. The process for accomplishing his task was simple: He was to review step by step any procedure being employed by the hospital and then, after careful examination of each of the steps, decide if the process could be improved.

The student arrived at the hospital not knowing where to begin. He telephoned his professor and asked the obvious question, "What do I do now?" He was again instructed to select an administrative procedure or process and track it to its logical conclusion. The student was still at a loss as to where to start; so the instructor, in some degree of frustration, told him to pick a bed sheet and follow that bed sheet step by step until he thoroughly understood what the hospital did with it. With that specific instruction the student began his labors. He identified the following steps:

1. After being used, the sheet was taken from the bed by a volunteer hospital worker. She threw the dirty sheet on the floor of the hospital corridor.

2. A man with a laundry cart gathered up all the soiled sheets from the floor and piled them into a bin constructed for that purpose. (Other men were doing similar work on the other eight floors of the hospital.)

3. Another man went from floor to floor, gathered up all the sheets, and took them to the basement.

4. In the basement the hospital had its own commercial laundry equipment. The sheets were laundered, ironed, and folded there by a team of workers.

5. The folded sheets were tied in bundles and delivered to the second floor storage room.

6. A nurse from each of the nine floors came to the storage room and took the number of sheets needed for her floor. She deposited these sheets in a small storage room on her floor.

7. A volunteer worker took the sheets from the small storage room and made the individual beds.

Could the process be shortened, modified, changed, or improved? While the analysis did not reveal any particular lack of stability, i.e., the soiled sheets were laundered and returned without crisis, some probable problems were identified and possible opportunities for the development of improved procedures (innovation) were noted:

1. Each sheet was individually handled by at least ten different people. (Too much duplication of effort.)
2. There was no need to tie the sheets in bundles. (It served no purpose.)
3. There was no need to have the second floor storage room. (The nurse could call down to the basement, ask for the number of sheets needed and the sheets could be delivered directly to the individual floors.)

After additional thought the student talked to personnel in other hospitals to see how they were handling their sheets. In one hospital he noticed that they had a laundry chute directly to the basement. All dirty sheets were merely taken from the beds and dropped into the chute. Could a similar small chute be constructed at his assigned hospital? He found that it could—and at a relatively low cost.

Now our student was becoming excited about his project. It had become more than just a task to complete for university credit. He was caught up with the concept that he could improve the system—that he could innovate. He talked to hospital service companies and, to his delight, found a company which made disposable bed sheets. Now he was really excited. He did a cost analysis to compare the current system against the proposed disposable sheet process. To his surprise, he found that if the hospital were to change to disposable sheets, it could save $100,000 in the first year's operation. He also found that the hospital could sell its laundry equipment for an additional $180,000. That, in turn, would free up an entire basement for other much-needed use. It was no surprise to find out that when that student made his remarkable presentation to the hospital administration, he was soon offered a very good position with them.

Let us examine the principal steps used by the student in the how-to-improve process. They were:

1. Identification of the current procedure or practice. (He tracked the process of laundering a bed sheet.)

2. Analysis of the procedures to find weak areas. (The student immediately found those areas which could easily be improved.)

3. Generation of ideas for improvement. (He first considered new procedures for those areas he found as being weak. He then investigated additional ways of accomplishing the task by talking to other hospital service agencies and so forth.)

4. Evaluation of new ideas. (He discussed his ideas with others, and he calculated costs, savings, and efficiency to see if his ideas were practical. Everything indicated that his new plan would dramatically improve the old system, so he presented his ideas to the hospital administration for implementation.)

5. Implementation of the ideas. (While the story does not detail the events of implementation, that process was accomplished.)

The five-point process for improvement worked for the student. Let's see now how the same points apply to missionary work.

My father, J. Layton Bishop, was one of the finest missionaries I have ever known. He was unable to go on a mission when he was a young man. Coming from a large family with only a widowed mother to support them, he was obligated to help maintain the family. He never lost his desire to serve on a mission, however, and after I returned from my first mission he and mother submitted their missionary papers and were called to serve in the Hawaiian Islands. Little did we know that father would give his life for that mission. His unrelenting drive soon provoked a rapid-beating heart, and he had to be sent home early from his mission. He lived only a few months more.

> Greater love hath no man than this, that a man lay down his life for his friends. (John 15:13.)

My father followed the previously mentioned steps in his quest to improve his mission.

1. *Identification of current procedure or practice.* My father was not a patient man. He was called to serve, and serve he did. He learned the mission programs quickly and started to work. At that time missionaries primarily knocked on doors to find people who were interested in the Church. That procedure was easy to learn and well known to all missionaries.

2. *Analysis of the procedures to find weak areas.* It did not take father long to note that the process was not giving him the results he wanted. As he knocked on doors, he found that few wanted to listen. He did not have time to waste on people who were not interested. He wanted to find those who were more in tune with the gospel principles.

3. *Generation of ideas for improvement.* He talked to other missionaries and listened to their ideas. The more he talked, the more he became convinced that there was a better way of finding the Lord's elect. He started looking for ways of meeting people who were better prepared for the gospel message. He wanted to find those who had already been exposed to the Church and who, while not yet baptized, were familiar and even in agreement with most or all the principles. The more he thought, the harder he prayed; the harder he prayed, the more he thought. One day the inspiration came to him.

4. *Evaluation of new ideas.* He rushed to the branch president and asked for a list of all the part-member families of the branch. He was amazed to discover how many there were. He found out everything he could about those families. He noted, for example, that there were army retirees and former business executives who frightened many of the younger missionaries. But he and mother were not to be frightened. They evaluated their plan to friend-ship these people until they knew of their sincere love for them. Father would be bold, mother would be loving; and they would teach them the gospel truths. They believed that their system would work.

5. *Implementation of new ideas.* Father put his plan into operation. He was determined that even if those long-time friends of
the Church had never listened to any other missionary, they
were going to listen to him. They made a great companionship
—mother, sweet and loving; father, bold and forceful. That
unique combination was soon producing more baptisms than
any other pair of missionaries in the mission. After their honest
love for the investigator was clearly established, dad would
corner the non-member and in straightforward language cry
repentance. These were people who were friends of the Church
but had never allowed missionaries to present the gospel message
in its depth. They did, however, listen to my father. Often the
non-member would later confess that he had just been waiting
for someone to come to tell him it was time to be baptized. The
maturity of my father in addition to his unique personality
qualified him for the task. He had desires that were beyond the
normal desire to serve. He had waited all his life for his chance
to serve, and he was going to do his best. That is precisely what
he did.

Note in this personal example that each of the five steps for
improving the finding process were clearly visible. As father
started to *identify* the on-going program of how to find the Lord's
elect, he *analyzed* the program and found it stable (in fact, it was
almost rigid). However, it did not provide the desired results at a
level compatible with his desires. He wanted faster results with
less expenditure of time. He simply reflected his goal against the
mission's standard program and found that it was inadequate to
satisfy his personal desires. Thus he identified a problem—the
difference between what he wanted (goal) and what was currently
being produced (results). He was naturally led to consider other
alternatives to achieve his desires.

That searching process *generated new ideas* in an innovative
way which resulted in the development of a unique plan. He and
mother carefully *evaluated* their plan, found it sound, and
implemented it. In this one effort they touched upon each of the
five steps which must be considered if one is to successfully
improve a system.

There are few successful missionaries who have not employed

these steps. They may not have known how to explain to others what they were doing, but the principles outlined above were always identified in their work.

In the more complex case of Elder Roberts, the efforts of an entire zone were involved in the improvement process. In this case also the five steps to mission improvement are of central importance.

Elder Roberts, a zone leader, was concerned that the level of efficiency and spirituality of his missionaries was not as high as it might be. He discussed these concerns with his district leaders and the missionaries in the districts and found that they agreed. Everyone felt that the mission as a whole had become comfortable at a mediocre level. Elder Roberts involved all of his missionaries in the discussion, and they unanimously agreed to become the model zone; by example, they would lift the efficiency and spirituality of the entire mission. They were one in their desire to improve their work and become better missionaries.

With that unanimous desire permeating their souls, Elder Roberts suggested that each missionary log his time and activities for the period of one week. He reasoned that they needed to know where they currently were, decide where they were going to be, and analyze how they might arrive there.

After each had carefully recorded his weekly activities, the leaders began to analyze. They discovered some startling information. Over 70 percent of the missionaries' time outside of their apartments was spent in travel. The missionaries had been trying to cover the entire area all at once. That practice forced the missionaries to waste valuable time as they traveled from discussion to discussion. Armed with that information, the missionaries organized their work areas into smaller segments. They selected those areas which were yielding the most baptisms and concentrated their efforts there, thus using valuable time which had been wasted in useless travel before. Almost overnight their baptisms increased dramatically.

Note that Elder Roberts was using the previously described process. Instead of identifying the individual steps in a specific missionary process, however, each missionary was identifying the steps in his everyday work habits. The results were the same.

Once one knows precisely what is being done, he finds that it can always be improved through careful evaluation and planning.

The missionaries also decided that their spirituality was the foundation of their capacity to find and baptize the Lord's elect. They used the same five-point process for improving their spirituality that they had used in improving their work habits. They first identified all of the things which they were doing to maintain their spirituality. In their analyses they found many areas which needed attention.

For example, many of the missionaries were reading newspapers and magazines which distracted their thinking from the work. They also noted that even an occasional movie on preparation day left them too often thinking of home. A few missionaries were even writing letters on days other than preparation day.

As the missionaries discussed these items in order to generate methods for improving their spirituality, they decided that perhaps they needed to develop their own zone "rules" to help them live on a higher spiritual level. They all agreed and unanimously established a new norm of missionary living, doing away with those things which distracted from the Spirit. It should be noted that they were prudent in their actions. They did not do anything contrary to established mission rules or anything that would endanger their health. They insisted that every missionary receive adequate rest and proper food, for example, because they understood the consequences of inappropriate sacrifice.

They adopted additional positive guidelines to help increase their spirituality. Scripture study was a must. Daily discussion review and improvement of their teaching technique became high on their list of priorities. They agreed to unitedly lift their voices in prayer at 6:30 A.M. from their respective apartments, praying for each other that the Lord's Spirit would be with them to direct their paths. They prayed especially for discernment, knowing that this gift was particularly important to their success. They prayed for the Lord's Spirit to be poured out in abundance upon the inhabitants of the city. After their "rules" or guidelines had been established, Elder Roberts took the list to the mission president for his consideration and approval. The president was impressed with the missionaries' dedication, their plans, and their work, and he gave his support and approval to all. His evaluation of their ideas was the missionaries' signal to implement their program.

Note again that the process to develop a successful mission was followed step by step as it related to only two issues: the missionaries' expenditure of time and their spirituality. In both cases they identified current procedures, analyzed for weaknesses, generated new ideas to improve the weak areas, evaluated the results of their efforts, and finally implemented that which was judged important. The Lord blessed them with insight, and a "new" zone soon took form. The results were astounding. When Elder Roberts started the identification process of current procedures, the zone of twenty missionaries was baptizing approximately twenty converts per month. Three months later, after much work and progress, the zone baptized over one hundred converts in a four-week period. Baptisms had quadrupled, and the converts remained active.

The other zones were still baptizing twenty people a month per zone, but now the other missionaries were talking. What was happening to Elder Roberts's zone and why? The example was too strong and too beautiful to be ignored. Other missionaries wanted to have similar success and thus implemented the same program.

Such action need not always start with a zone. It may start with two missionaries or the entire mission. The principles, however, are always the same. To succeed, one need only apply them appropriately.

Each missionary should check his ability to identify the major characteristics of a successful mission as well as the steps that Elder Roberts and my father used in improving their missions. Then when the opportunity presents itself, the missionary is prepared to implement the process in his own work.

Missionaries should remember that whatever is being done can be improved. There is a better way to do it. Find that way.

Chapter 13

Members As Finders
of the Lord's Elect

In section 84 of the Doctrine and Covenants the Lord indicates that he would forgive the sins of those to whom the revelation was addressed and commanded them to steadfastly bear testimony to the world of the gospel light he had given them (verse 61); he then declared the signs that would follow those who believe (verses 65-72), indicated for whom the gospel is intended (verse 75), and finally noted who is responsible to accomplish the work (verse 76). The Lord says that the burden of missionary work rests upon the members of the Church, "unto *all* those to whom the kingdom has been given." He makes no distinction between full-time missionaries and other members of the Church. Each is expected to do his or her part. For orderly coordination, however, the Church has assigned the primary role of teaching the gospel to the missionaries, while the members are encouraged to find appropriate candidates for them to teach.

In missions where the Church program is fully established, the full-time missionaries carefully coordinate their activities through the ward mission director, the bishopric, and other ward leaders. In harmonious interaction, the full-time missionaries report their labors and needs, and member families are assigned to assist in the work. In missions which are not yet fully developed, a missionary may have to function as branch president and branch mission leader. In such cases the missionaries must arrange and coordinate all missionary functions between themselves and the members. In these situations the full-time missionary must stimulate and gain missionary support from the members if a united missionary effort is to be established.

Many missionaries falsely assume that if they are friends with the members, this automatically implies that the members have confidence in them. Experience has proven, however, that the fundamental factor in whether members entrust their non-member friends to the full-time missionaries is the degree of confidence they have in the missionaries as competent teachers and emissaries of the gospel of salvation. The existing degree of that trust determines the degree to which the member will contribute his efforts to the missionary work. There is no other variable so important.

Obviously missionaries need to be great teachers, both by exemplary living and by performance in teaching situations. They must remain somewhat distant from the things of the world and be involved only in missionary work. Specifically, missionaries may appropriately take the following steps to increase the members' confidence in them. These might be referred to as the "ten commandments" for missionary visits to members.

1. *Make every visit to the members a spiritual experience.* The missionary who merely goes to the members and asks, "Do you have any referrals for us today?" is missing a significant opportunity. On the other hand, the missionary who consciously develops his message in advance, who gives the family a spiritual, learning experience with his visits, is successful. It takes little imagination to know that those member families soon will be stimulated to noble activity in missionary work because of how they feel about those quality missionaries. There is no better way to gain member confidence than by provocative demonstration of the missionary's teaching ability.

2. *Visit missionary-minded members regularly.* This concept is given as a general guideline. There may be occasions when, for prudent reasons, a missionary would want to visit a particular family often and occasions when he may not want to visit nearly

so frequently. The concept, however, is that missionaries are to pay special weekly attention to those members who are actively engaged in the finding process of missionary work and give them moral and spiritual support.

But the term *visit* can be misleading. It must not be construed to mean that the missionary enters the member's home, sits down, and engages in casual conversation with the member. To the contrary, missionaries must always be careful not to make such "visits." The intelligent missionary controls that situation by being well organized and prepared with his message and quickly directs the conversation into a spiritual path.

3. *Bless the home of the member.* Missionaries should pray for and with the members they visit. This is an integral part of the desired spiritual experience but unfortunately it is often forgotten. When missionaries teach the gospel to investigators, they always pray with them; but after the family is baptized, that kneeling prayer is sometimes forgotten. Thus, the members are left feeling that now that they are members of the Church, the missionaries are no longer concerned about their spiritual welfare. They rightly feel that they are not treated as well as when they were investigating the Church. Pray with them and for them, whether they are new members or old members, and if at all possible, have everyone kneel for that prayer.

4. *Keep visits short and to the point.* Missionaries can teach the members the importance of the work by their actions. For example, the missionary who has time to waste in a member's home is signaling that there is no real urgency in doing missionary work. If there is no urgency on the part of the missionary, there will be little urgency on the part of the member to accomplish his own missionary goals. But the missionary who is excited and obviously busy in the Lord's work will convey the appropriate message to the member.

5. *Stay away from social themes.* Missionaries should keep the discussion directed to the purpose of their prepared lesson as much as possible. This not only renders direction but also keeps missionaries from becoming inappropriately involved in controversial topics. They particularly must not become involved in any of the ward or branch problems.

6. *Avoid eating with members during these visits.* While the missionary must be careful not to display bad manners on these visits, his gently declining to eat will reaffirm in the mind of all the purpose of the visit—to find people to teach. If that purpose is undermined or subtly replaced in any way, if the member comes to feel that the "real" purpose of the visit is something other than *urgent missionary work*, that member will not reach his or her potential as a member missionary, and the missionary will not be as effective.

7. *Avoid chastising members in manner or words for their lack of support in the missionary work.* It is not appropriate for the missionaries to belittle members or make them feel guilty for their lack of support. Do not use scripture or messages from General Authorities which could be interpreted as a scolding or preachment. Focus instead on goals which can only be interpreted as being positive. Remember that love begets love. An offended member is unproductive and is a negative influence in the work.

8. *Teach the members appropriate aspects of missionary work by example, precept, and a happy disposition.* Not all members are alike. Some have natural talents in all phases of missionary work relative to finding the elect. Others struggle to say good morning to a stranger. The task of the missionary is to assist the member in identifying missionary work goals that are realistic and at the same time challenging. That task must be done with a happy disposition so that the family's spirits are lifted and a feeling of joy abounds.

9. *Avoid entering into discussions with the members relative to their personal problems or problems that may exist between them and other Church members.* The missionary is to do proselyting work. He has been called full-time to do so. He is not called or authorized to listen to or solve intimate personal problems. He should direct the member to discuss these issues with the appropriate priesthood leader.

10. *Leave as soon as your message and missionary goal have been established.* Often the testifying Spirit of our Heavenly Father is evidenced during the missionaries' message. If missionaries leave immediately after that message has been delivered, the members will note that the Spirit also dissipates shortly afterwards. They

will recognize that the missionaries were responsible for having delivered a message which carried the testimony of the Spirit. That confirmation will provoke increased confidence in the missionaries and an increased desire on the part of the member to more productively participate in missionary work.

There is an underlying concept in the preceding ten guidelines which should not be overlooked—*the automatic increase in work force* when members become actively engaged in missionary work. Missionaries can generate a major expansion in the work through their training efforts with the members. The missionary who develops the Spirit within him and a skill in provoking the members to become happily and productively engaged in missionary work will proportionately reduce his own work load relative to finding and friendshipping investigators. He is freed to concentrate his efforts on teaching the gospel. Clearly, the missionary who is engaged full-time in teaching will double or triple the number of convert baptisms over those other missionaries who are left to spend a major portion of their time looking for the elusive, interested contact.

Working with members is one of the primary principles for finding the Lord's elect. Build upon it.

Chapter 14

Missionaries As Finders

By revelation the Lord commands his missionaries to open their mouths and teach the gospel.

> Open your mouths and they shall be filled, and you shall become even as Nephi of old, who journeyed from Jerusalem in the wilderness.
>
> Yea, open your mouths and spare not, and you shall be laden with sheaves upon your backs, for lo, I am with you.
>
> Yea, open your mouths and they shall be filled, saying: Repent, repent, and prepare ye the way of the Lord, and make his paths straight; for the kingdom of heaven is at hand. (D&C 33:8-10.)

After each commandment comes the statement of the blessing. This divine revelation directs the faithful missionary. Obedience to the Lord's holy will seals the promise.

To obey this commandment and to do it well is one of the major tasks one has in the mission field. To be successful, missionaries must learn to open their mouths and to do so in the right fashion. Inevitably there are those missionaries who are shy. It frightens them to think about approaching strangers and engaging them in conversation, particularly concerning religion. Logically, before a missionary can learn how to find the Lord's elect, he has to learn how to meet and to talk to strangers about the gospel. Fortunately, there are simple, specific steps in that learning process. One needs only to apply himself to the task with sincerity.

A Three-Step Formula for Finding Investigators

The initial step is to be mentally prepared. The missionary has nothing to fear. It is not he who is being called to repentance. If there is any fear in this process, it more appropriately rests with the nonbeliever. The missionary should remember who he literally represents and have no fear. People may shut the door in the face of a missionary, or they may say that they do not want to hear about the Church. The missionary simply must say in his or her mind, *Well, I am sorry for you; but there is someone else nearby who is waiting for my message. My task is to find him.*

An additional step for missionaries to remember as they are preparing themselves mentally is to smile. Happy missionaries, by virtue of their enthusiasm, excite people to want to know more. A contagious enthusiasm is what makes missionaries successful in meeting people. If greetings are said with a smile, no one can be upset.

The third step in this process is to go from smiling and being happy to greeting the people. Elder Spencer, an outstanding missionary in Argentina, passed by a little old lady one morning and said, "Good morning, how are you?" She responded, "Young man, I don't know you, do I?" Then he said, "No, you don't know me, but where I am from we always say hello to people we pass in the street. It just makes everyone feel good, don't you think?" And she turned and said to him, "Why, I believe you are right!" The next morning he came out of his apartment and he ran into her again. Guess who was the first one to say good morning? It was, of course, the little old lady. His cheery hello had prepared the way. It cultivated the lady's mind to be friendly. Missionaries who are friendly teach other people to be friendly.

Remember the equation:

PROPER MENTAL PREPARATION + A WINNING SMILE
+ AN ABILITY TO GREET THE PEOPLE
= A FOUNDATION FOR MISSIONARY SUCCESS

It is well to note that the missionary who is sent to a foreign-speaking mission will not find it a disadvantage to be struggling with the language. The native people often want so much to help the "poor" new missionary that they draw him into their hearts. As the new missionary struggles with the language, the people come to his rescue; of course, the missionary can then go to theirs, offering the way to salvation and life eternal.

After the missionary has learned the above three basic steps, the rest is relatively easy. He merely continues, directing the conversation toward the purpose of his calling. For example, after the missionary has greeted the person, he may simply and directly explain who he is and what he is doing. Missionaries trying to find a reference, for example, will often stop to knock at any door in the neighborhood and ask if they know where such-and-such a family lives. After they respond, the missionary may say, "We are missionaries of The Church of Jesus Christ of Latter-day Saints, and we are visiting this family because they asked us to come to their home. We have a message for all families and it deals with. . . ." Then the missionary finishes his explanation.

The process may start off with a question, "Good morning, could you help us?" Then the missionaries ask their question relevant to their work. "Could you tell us who moved into this neighborhood recently? Do you know anyone who is newly married? who had a baby? or who had a recent death in the family?"

Ofttimes missionaries miss an ideal opportunity to strike up a natural conversation with someone about the gospel. I remember when our family went downtown in Buenos Aires to celebrate our son's birthday. As we were returning in the train, my youngest son, Scotty, gave me a big hug. Not to be outdone, my fifteen-year-old son, Steven, came over and did the same. I was standing in the train, rocking along; my wife was holding tightly onto my arm and gaily chatting about the events of the evening. Finally, my older son, Michael, taller than I, walked over to my side and thanked me for the nice evening he had had on his birthday, punctuating his feeling with a hug. Only a few moments later a complete stranger came over, extended his hand to me, and said, "My, what a lovely family you have!" He had opened a conversation with that compliment. But I was so taken by surprise that I missed a beautiful opportunity to explain more to him of who we were. The only thing I could think of to say to him was "Thank you very much." The point is that a sincere compliment to a parent about his or her children goes directly to the parent's heart. A missionary needs to learn to take advantage of this. When a missionary is around people, he must learn to talk. For example, "It's a beautiful day," or "My, what a lovely family you have!" or, "Do you know where this family lives?" As the missionary is friendly with people, he finds that they generally respond in the same friendly, sincere manner in which they are approached.

Elder Tuckett was a farm boy who, although somewhat shy, was endowed with a natural, easygoing missionary manner which drew people to him. He always had a smile on his face which went well indeed with his disarming boyish countenance. He obviously loved people and enjoyed talking to them. He was what some might refer to as the all-American boy. His boyish features were compatible with his manly ways, and he capitalized on his natural talents to help him do the Lord's work.

Although Elder Tuckett had baptisms almost weekly, his proselyting hours, as compiled in the president's weekly report, were not good. As a matter of fact, they were terrible. The obvious question was how Elder Tuckett could have so many baptisms if he was not capable of finding investigators. In his interviews with the president, Elder Tuckett was evasive about how he found contacts; he would always talk about his investigators and their children rather than how he found them. When asked directly how he became acquainted with a specific family, he would take no credit for finding them. Instead he would indicate that they seemed to "fall out of the trees" (an expression missionaries often used to describe a direct blessing from our Father in Heaven).

Several interviews took place before the total finding process was finally clarified by Elder Tuckett's companion. It seemed that Elder Tuckett had identified three member families who loved to visit with everyone. He had established a great rapport with these families and a mutual love evolved. He had then organized the "Elder Tuckett system of cultivating and finding the Lord's elect." He would merely visit each of these families in rotation. Upon his arrival, the children of the family would visit a neighbor family or two, indicating that the mother wanted them to come and visit over a cup of mate (a South American drink offered customarily in social situations comparable to the North American coffee break). When the neighbors arrived, the member would introduce Elder Tuckett and his companion as "missionaries from our church," and a friendly atmosphere always prevailed as the casual conversation took place.

Elder Tuckett had an ability to listen and interact with people in such a way as to teach the gospel. Often he would refer to his "daddy's teachings" when he was back on the farm (of course, his "daddy's teachings" were founded upon the teachings of the Savior). On occasions, he would give an entire informal missionary discussion without the people ever knowing that a specific lesson was in process. He referred to these "chats" as his way of preparing or cultivating the person for the formal lessons. His process of preparation seemed to naturally lead the people to want to know about the gospel. As a natural result, he and his companion were invited to the homes of these new contacts to meet friends and relatives so they too might "chat" with this affable young man from the United States.

This seemingly casual process was, in fact, very structured. Elder Tuckett had trained his member families to do missionary work according to their natural friendshipping abilities. They were not hesitant to help because it was something they were used to doing and could do well. He merely structured an existing situation to provide teaching opportunities and then capitalized on his unique talents to teach the message of salvation. Although few missionaries come into the mission field as prepared to fill such specifically designed tasks, each can apply the same principle. Each can design the task of cultivating and developing relationships to fit his talents. The extent to which he is able to do this is the extent to which he will be a successful finding missionary.

The case of Sister Jackson represents another good example of using one's talents. Sister Jackson was the envy of every missionary in her mission. She consistently brought contacts to baptisms and always had several investigator families attending Church every Sunday. She was able to find new families seemingly without effort. She regarded her area of labor as very blessed and more productive than any other area. When transferred into a new and less productive area, she soon changed the area to reach the productive level of her old area.

She stated over and over that she had no specific system. Careful analysis, however, demonstrated the contrary. Instinctively, Sister Jackson and her companion concentrated their efforts in a small ten-by-seven-block area. The two sisters walked back and forth through this small area many times every day. The process seemed completely unplanned, but it clearly reflected the personalities and talents of both sisters. They were friendly and outgoing. Their behavior was that of a good neighbor. They said hello to everyone in their small area, and soon everyone was their friend. Their introduction of the gospel was natural and unstrained. Their teachings in the beginning stages were more exemplary than formal. They referred to this process as "cultivating"; however, their goal was never forgotten. The intent was first to establish a strong base by their example and then to teach as the occasion would permit.

A key factor in their success was that they concentrated their efforts in a relatively small sector and they were seen often, sometimes two or three times a day by the same person. They soon became well known because they were so friendly—always being the first to say hello or to help someone home with her groceries. After approximately two weeks of their making friends with the people in this fashion, everyone began to ask what it was that they were doing. Because they were such fine, outstanding young ladies, they were soon invited into homes to explain their message. Because of their kindness, coupled with their naturally happy way of life, many wanted to know more.

Soon the sisters were spending most of their time teaching, leaving the task of cultivating the people for when they walked to and from their discussions. As baptisms came, more people became interested, and more people were introduced to the sisters. Soon everyone knew them, respected them, and loved them. They cultivated their small area with love and example until the harvest was ripe. They referred to it as their "mini-Zion." Is it any wonder that other "mini-Zion" sectors soon were developed by other missionaries throughout the mission?

The concept that love begets love is a sound principle that is worthy of modeling by others. "Love thy neighbor as thyself," is the foundation. Use it. It works.

Finding the Elect Through Investigators

Investigators do not all have the same level of commitment to The Church of Jesus Christ of Latter-day Saints. They are, after all, still investigating. Nevertheless, their commitment to investigate the Church is probably sufficient for them to recommend that others do the same.

An inquiry as to who among the investigator's friends and family might also be interested in the gospel can be used appropriately in virtually all the missionary discussions. For example, from past experience we know the gospel often appeals to those who are experiencing changes in their lives. The missionary should always be searching for such individuals with questions directed to his investigator: "Who do you know who recently was married?" "Who do you know who recently had a baby?" "Who do you know who recently had a death in the family?" Or simply, "Who do you know who needs the gospel?"

The missionary should not ask these questions casually. With pad and pencil in hand he should be ready to take down names and addresses. That clear signal underscores the intent of the questions. It will provoke serious reflection on the part of the investigator to carefully consider the request rather than brush it aside carelessly.

Should the investigator wish his name to be used as you visit his referral, the additional support renders strength in entering the new homes. If the investigator is reluctant, however, the missionary should most carefully respect his desires and wishes.

Occasionally, an investigator may wish to invite friends or relatives to his home to hear the next discussion. This is a blessing and at the same time a dilemma. Should the missionary give the second lesson to all who attend, recognizing that full understanding depends in part upon having received the first lesson? Should the first lesson be presented again so that the group may progress together? Should the missionaries develop a third lesson designed especially for the occasion? Should they turn to films, such as "Man's Search for Happiness" or "The First Vision"?

There is no definitive answer other than that the missionaries should follow the dictates of the Spirit and go forth fully prepared to present their message. No missionary should enter into that kind of meeting unprepared and wait for the Spirit to descend. While such an experience may occur, the prayerful, dedicated missionary will usually be inspired as to which direction he should take and can be totally prepared prior to the meeting.

Investigators often have strong testimonies of the gospel of Jesus Christ and fully desire to share these precious truths with all who will listen. Such an investigator needs only some general guidelines and instruction on how to proceed. It is for the missionary to provide that specific instruction to the investigator as to what missionary functions he should consider. But missionaries should take care not to jeopardize the investigator's own development. Generally speaking, the steps outlined by President Kimball are appropriate for both converted investigators and members relative to finding more investigators. Those steps are:

1. Prepare a list of families which may be interested in the gospel.
2. Prayerfully select one or two families to friendship according to the direction of the Spirit.
3. Invite the families to the home to receive a message from the missionaries.

Often the investigator will already have gone through the first steps of this process. Obviously the selected families then need only to be invited to a missionary family home evening.

Investigators can be one of the missionary's most valuable resources in finding more people to teach. Not to utilize that resource appropriately would indeed be a serious mistake.

Chapter 15

Teaching, Baptizing, and Fellowshipping the Lord's Elect

It is the Spirit of the Lord, not the missionary, that converts the honest in heart. It is also evident, however, that a successful missionary will employ those methods, skills, techniques, persuasions, and discussions which will provide the best possible conditions for the Spirit to witness and testify. It is logical and reasonable for the missionary to use teaching techniques, body language, faith, love, inspiration, and actions in a carefully orchestrated sequence so that the investigator clearly understands the gospel message.

Missionaries teach to enable the investigator to have knowledge—knowledge to which the missionaries bear testimony. Eternal truths are declared to the investigator, but they are of little value to him until he believes them. That belief occurs precisely when the investigator receives and accepts the witness of the Holy Spirit. When the Spirit speaks to spirit, conversion takes place. Confirmation of the holy experience occurs when the investigator bears his testimony back to the missionaries. That exchange of truth is the purpose and design of missionary work. Everything that is said or done should have that end in mind.

Guidelines for Preparing and Teaching Investigators

Each mission has its own programs designed to address its unique needs. In like manner the Church has appropriately established for all missions a uniform system of teaching the gospel of Jesus Christ. The following eleven guidelines are compatible with both individual and mission programs wherever they may be, as well as with the Church uniform system of teaching. If followed carefully, the guidelines will render sound assistance and positive results to missionaries wherever they may serve. These concepts are tried and proven and reflect basic gospel principles.

1. *Visit daily.* When possible, missionaries should visit their investigators daily. The missionaries need not enter the home during these visits. If they do, they should stay only a few minutes—just long enough to leave a prayer, a cheery word, a thought for the day, and some sentiments of gospel love. This expression of caring engenders a reciprocal spirit of love. Cultivation of gospel love prepares the spirit of the investigator to be able to receive the spiritual witness when the appropriate time comes.

2. *Be spiritually prepared.* The Savior gave us a model account of spiritual preparation when he fasted forty days and nights in order to prepare himself for that glorious event that eventually brought forgiveness and redemption within our grasp if we are but faithful. While it is not necessary or appropriate for the missionary to fast before every discussion, it is appropriate for him to strengthen himself spiritually.

For example, humble prayer before leaving the missionaries' quarters is normal procedure. It is also appropriate for the missionaries to speak in subdued tones as they near an investigator's home, reverently contemplating the need for the Lord's witness and of their own reliance upon him. They should carry an additional prayer in their hearts prior to actually entering the investigator's home. Additional preparations should also be considered by the individual missionary as his spirit and conscience dictates. The point is simple: Missionaries should be fully pre-pared spiritually for every discussion. That phase of missionary work should never become routine. There are too many souls in the balance. The responsibilities are too great for the missionary to become careless or complacent.

3. *Kneel in prayer with the investigators.* There may be occa-sions when a kneeling prayer is inappropriate, but generally speaking the missionary should try to arrange for the family to kneel in prayer. There is added reverence which vibrates through the soul on such occasions. The missionaries' task is to add to each discussion every spiritual element that is within his scope of understanding and reach.

Sister Redona, an excellent missionary and a spiritual giant, demonstrated in her farewell interview her depth of understand-ing concerning kneeling prayer. She was discussing some of the events of her mission and was relating some of her more spiritual experiences when she stopped suddenly and reverently slipped to her knees as if to pray. She looked up at me still seated in my chair watching her and said, "Oh, President, please forgive me! It is just that I am so accustomed to kneeling in prayer with my investigators when I feel the Spirit that I did so without think-ing." Her eyes laughing, she continued, "I guess you're not an investigator, are you?"

What a sense of pride I felt on that occasion! Oh that all missionaries might someday arrive at the point of automatically kneeling when the Spirit is present, thus inviting others to join! That missionary had learned the signal. She had the faith to know that the Lord would answer the sincere heart, that her task was to assist others, giving them the confidence to ask if the Book of Mormon is true, if Joseph Smith was indeed a prophet, and so forth. With unshakable faith she led her families in kneeling prayer to receive their own witness. Is it any wonder that she led the mission in the number of convert baptisms? She saw the power of kneeling prayer and used it. All missionaries should do the same.

4. *Point out the Spirit.* For investigators who have never had spiritual experiences before, a witness of the Spirit is not always understood. Since the missionary's desire is that the investigator

receive confirmation of the truths of the gospel, he should be alert and sensitive to the Spirit. Often the missionaries sense the presence of the Spirit during their discussion but fail to specifically draw the investigator's attention to it. On such occasions, the missionaries should stop speaking, hesitate a few seconds to gain the attention of all present, and explain that the peaceful joy all are experiencing is the blessing of the Holy Ghost. Then, depending upon the dictates of the Spirit, the missionaries may choose to kneel in prayer, as Sister Redona frequently did, or simply indicate that as the investigator continues to search for the truth he will experience additional spiritual feelings to testify to that which he hears, reads, ponders, and particularly that for which he prays. The missionaries may focus additional instructions on the non-member's need for preparation to become worthy to receive confirmation of his petitions. The missionaries may then appropriately return to their discussion for the evening.

5. *Present message as revealed through Joseph Smith and latter-day revelation.* The Lord has stated clearly that we should teach his word as it has been revealed through Joseph Smith (D&C 5:10). In speaking on this issue, Elder Bruce R. McConkie stated to a group of new mission presidents:

> It has been our traditional course in days past, unfortunately all too frequently, to say, "Here is the Bible, and the Bible says this and this, and therefore the gospel has been restored." Well now, there is no person on earth that believes the Bible more than I do. I read it and ponder its words. I know that what is in it is true. But let me tell you, it is not the Bible that brings people into the Church; it is the Book of Mormon and latter-day revelation. We can use the Bible to lay a foundation, and to point people's attention to Joseph Smith and the Book of Mormon, but until we get involved with latter-day revelation, the processes of conversion do not begin to operate in any substantial degree in the heart of an investigator. The Lord said to Joseph Smith: "This generation shall have my word through you." (D&C 5:10.)
>
> This is his decree. They either get it through Joseph Smith or they do not get it, and our whole perspective is: Joseph Smith and the Book of Mormon, the Book of Mormon and Joseph Smith. The Bible and all else that we have is to shore up, and to point the direction. . . .

The message of the Restoration is three things—it is the divine Sonship of Christ, it is the divine mission of the Prophet Joseph Smith, and it is the truth and divinity of the Church. You know and can analyze it out that the Book of Mormon is given to prove that Jesus is the Christ. It also proves that Joseph Smith is a prophet; and out of that grows the divinity of the Church. When people believe in Christ and in Joseph Smith and in the divinity of the Church, and desire to do right, we want to baptize them. (Mission Presidents Seminar, June 21, 1975.)

The distinguishing characteristic of the Lord's one and only true Church is that it is founded by him upon the rock of continuing revelation. The Lord once again spoke through his prophets. It is no wonder that we are to lay our foundation upon that rock of revelation and proceed as the Lord deemed necessary—to proclaim the gospel as restored through the Prophet Joseph; that is, modern revelation.

6. *Bear testimony.* Some missionaries become locked into the missionary discussions. The discussion is not to be given mechanically. It is to lead to the witness. If the Spirit is strongly felt, the missionary should stop, wait a few seconds to give emphasis to what has been said, and then bear testimony. At that point the Spirit will confirm what has been said, and the investigator should be invited to express his feelings. The missionary must build upon those feelings so the investigator will know that he has a testimony and that it is growing stronger day by day. Remember, missionaries are sent out to both teach and to testify. And that testimony must be sincere and humble, and whenever possible it should reflect personal experiences. If it is part of a memorized script it will not be received with deep spiritual understanding by the investigator.

7. *Help the investigator understand the strength of his testimony.* Investigators often have the misconception that a testimony must come as a sudden witness from on high, particularly if the missionaries fail to teach them about the Spirit (as discussed in number four of this section). Sometimes investigators fail to realize that the whispering of the still small voice has borne witness to them and that they already have the foundation of a testimony.

It is the missionary's responsibility to sharply focus the attention of the investigator on the significant elements of his testimony. To do so, missionaries should ask the following two basic questions:

A. Do you believe that the Book of Mormon is the word of God, as reported through the record of the ancient inhabitants of the American continent—engraved upon plates of gold and hidden away for centuries—to come forth as was announced in the Bible and to later be translated by the power of God through Joseph Smith? Or is it fiction? It is either one or the other. Which do you believe it is?

B. Do you believe that Joseph Smith was a prophet of God raised up in these latter days to fulfill biblical prophecies and to reestablish the true church of Jesus Christ upon the face of the earth? Or was Joseph Smith a fraud? He has to be one or the other. Which do you believe?

Such clearly delineated distinctions almost always cause the investigator to realize that he does indeed believe the Book of Mormon to be the word of God—that the book could not have been written by man and that Joseph Smith was indeed a prophet. With that realization and spiritual confirmation, the investigator needs to understand that a basic testimony is already his. He is then better prepared to accept additional truths.

8. *Leave the investigator's home quickly after the missionary discussion.* This guideline was previously cited relative to missionaries working with members. The concept is the same when working with investigators, because the workings of the Spirit are the same. The Spirit testifies, blesses, and strengthens, and brings peace, joy, and happiness. Missionaries who want their work always to be associated with the labor of the Spirit should understand that the Spirit is there primarily to testify of their message. Once that task has been completed, the Spirit will depart. The missionary should leave also so that the investigator realizes that when the missionaries teach and testify, the Spirit is present to render holy confirmation. The investigator should always associate missionaries with spiritual experiences. Missionaries who linger after a spiritual feast to enter into discussions of social or worldly themes may destroy the good impressions they have

created and damage their credibility in the mind of the investigator.

Also, missionaries should depart from the home reverently. Some missionaries make the terrible mistake of saying something to each other in a loud voice as they walk away from the door. Even a positive statement, such as "Wasn't that a great discussion, Elder?" can be misunderstood if all the investigator hears are loud voices as the missionaries leave. The investigator may feel the missionaries are making fun of him. The missionary should always remember that spiritual experiences are new for the investigators. Constant vigilance by the missionaries is prudent if they are not to be misunderstood.

9. *Give thanks.* Missionaries pray often to ask for the Lord's support. The prophet Alma instructed us to give thanks also. He said: "And now I would that ye should be humble, and be submissive and gentle; easy to be entreated; full of patience and long-suffering; being temperate in all things; being diligent in keeping the commandments of God at all times; asking for whatsoever things ye stand in need, both spiritual and temporal; *always returning thanks unto God for whatsoever things ye do receive.*" (Alma 7:23; emphasis added.)

It is appropriate for missionaries to give special prayers of thanks as the occasion might warrant. Specifically, after spiritual experiences a prayer of sincere gratitude fortifies the spirit and helps us maintain a close relationship with the Lord, who divinely directs our paths.

10. *Be bold.* Strength and conviction in our revealed knowledge is power unto salvation for those who will but listen. When a speaker knows what he is talking about, when he is absolutely convinced that what he is saying is true, and when he delivers his message with the power of his conviction, people generally listen. These three elements must come together in balance and harmony.

Missionaries know of what they speak. They have diligently studied the restored gospel of Jesus Christ. They also have personal, sacred testimonies of the truth of their message. It only remains for them to be bold in the delivery of their message to the convincing of those who will listen.

The statement should not be misinterpreted as a license to be offensive, rude, arrogant, or ill-mannered. Boldness underscores such words as dedication, conviction, importance, urgency, concern, and love unfeigned. Many non-members are waiting for someone with love abounding to tell them, "It's time for you to be baptized—you have waited long enough." Boldness tempered with love is the key to that person's baptism.

11. *Prepare the investigators to remain active after their baptisms.* The process of integrating new members into the Church is socially complex. New members view the wonders of the gospel, see its love radiating from the missionaries, feel the confirmation of the Spirit, and believe they have encountered perfection on earth. In truth, they are correct in their assumption—as it relates to the Church. It is perfect. In no other structure, concept, or rationale is purpose and destiny so gloriously and perfectly proclaimed as it is in The Church of Jesus Christ of Latter-day Saints.

Unfortunately the same level of perfection does not yet exist in the lives of the members. We are yet mortal; but the investigator and recently baptized member hold fast to the expectation that since the Church is perfect, in like manner the Saints must be perfect.

They must understand that the Church exists

> For the perfecting of the saints, for the work of the ministry, for the edifying of the body of Christ:
> Till we all come in the unity of the faith, and of the knowledge of the Son of God, unto a perfect man, unto the measure of the stature of the fulness of Christ. (Ephesians 4:12-13.)

Operationally the Church resembles a hospital for the spiritually sick. Sinners from all walks of life enter through the door of baptism and begin to become whole. This healing process is generally line upon line and precept upon precept. Some are "cured" almost overnight and quickly develop a finite perfection. Others have more lingering spiritual diseases which require life-long support and understanding before they are able to but walk. There are others who seem to function well until the hidden cancer of sin finally takes the soul of that individual as he dies a spiritual death and is excommunicated from the Lord's kingdom.

Missionaries must prepare their investigators to understand that the purpose of the Church is "for the perfecting of the Saints" and assist them to participate in that process by keeping the Lord's counsel:

> Thou shalt love the Lord thy God with all thy heart, and with all thy soul, and with all thy mind.
> And the second is like unto it, Thou shalt *love thy neighbour as thyself.* (Matthew 22:37, 39; emphasis added.)

Some investigators and recently baptized members become inactive because they are offended by the real or perceived actions of a member. To prevent such an eventuality, missionaries must prepare their investigators by teaching them basic concepts of forgiving others, supporting the unit leaders, and not judging others. Each missionary can relate to them how a faithful member who, for one silly reason or another, left the Church. Church leaders, witnesses to the Book of Mormon, and members offended by a bishop, for example, have all left their sad personal histories behind as a trail of bones on the road of error. Point them out to the investigator so that he might be forewarned and forearmed.

It seems prudent also to explain to investigators that some who claim to have had bad experiences with leaders or members often have their own cancerous imperfections hidden deep inside. Blaming others is tantamount to covering up personal weaknesses and soothing one's own conscience, as it were. In the final analysis a man's sins will be made visible, for his judgment will inevitably come due as it will for all of the Saints.

In speaking to Peter, the Lord said: "But I have prayed for thee, that thy faith fail not: *and when thou art converted, strengthen thy brethren.*" (Luke 22:32; emphasis added.) Not only should investigators understand that they are to overlook the mistakes of others, but also that they, as healthy members, are to strengthen their brethren. Theirs is to lift up, to understand, to love, and to work together until we all come to the unity of the faith and love our neighbors as ourselves.

It is extremely important that people are not baptized and then forgotten, for such soon will become inactive. Experienced missionaries as well as the local leaders will track the progress of their converts, being continually aware of their activity so that the appropriate transition from the missionary to the seasoned members takes place.

The two main indicators of missionary success are the number of convert baptisms and the continued activity (retention) of those converts in the Church. To focus primarily on one of these indicators and ignore the other is a serious mistake. A proper balance must take place. Those missionaries who think only of baptisms and care not if the converts remain active or whether they have been adequately prepared to remain active, do an injustice to the convert. To the contrary, the missionary who fails to baptize the convert when the heartfelt conversion has taken place and prolongs the teaching process to be certain the investigator is beyond any doubt totally ready also does an injustice to the investigator. The investigator who has felt the witness of the Spirit and desires baptism rarely becomes inactive if after baptism the assimilation process into membership is done continually and carefully.

There are, of course, more principles of teaching the elect than the eleven briefly mentioned here. All, however, are based upon revealed truth. These few are given as guidelines only. The Spirit will assist the dedicated missionary in recognizing other equally important teaching techniques.

What to Do When a Golden Family Changes Their Mind

There may be occasions when an outstanding, seemingly spiritual investigator family, without warning, will announce in tones of a definitive decision that they no longer desire to have any affiliation with the true church of God. The missionary should be prepared for such an occasion with a preconceived counteraction. He should not yield to the normal tendency to express confused regrets and leave.

Such occurrences take place because someone or something has prevailed against the Spirit and has momentarily confused the investigator to the point of withdrawal. To effectively combat such a dazed state of mind, the missionary must assemble some point of order and tranquility into the discussion, or he will fail. For such occasions there are procedures which can provide some order and give the missionary time to assess the situation, identify the reasons for the sudden change, and discern what should be done to bring that soul back into the fold.

Assume for a moment that the worthy father meets the missionary at the door with the Book of Mormon and some Church pamphlets in his hand. He states that the family wants nothing more to do with the Church and they are returning the previously mentioned materials. What should the missionary do? In this particular case it is first a question of what he should not do. He should not reach out to take the materials but, rather, should ignore the fact that they are being extended to him. The investigator's arm will soon tire and retreat to his side.

While the investigator is trying to terminate the relationship in the doorway, the missionary should in peaceful tones indicate his surprise at the decision. He then might say something which could appropriately resemble the following: "Brother Brown, while we are greatly surprised that you do not wish to study the Church anymore, we recognize that it is your right to decide to continue or not. We, of course, will abide by your decision. However, we have become most fond of you and your family. Would you, therefore, permit us to come in and visit for a moment or at least say good-bye?"

Since the request is honest and filled with unfeigned love toward the family, it is normally granted. The father is still holding the materials, and the missionaries are invited in. At this point the missionary should demonstrate love unfeigned and attempt to slow down the events of the evening in order to arrive at the real reason the family has taken such a negative position.

The basis of the investigator's rejection of the gospel of Jesus Christ normally can be attributed to the influence of others who are misinformed and have been directed to the investigator by the adversary. These misguided souls have temporarily convinced the investigator to separate himself from the truth. Often missionaries will find that the fateful decision is not representative of the whole family, but of the feelings of perhaps just one member of the family.

After the missionaries have successfully demonstrated their sincere affection for each member of the family and told them how they will miss their weekly visits, the senior companion should carefully begin to probe for the hidden reason for the abrupt turn of events. The following pattern might be followed: "Brother Brown, as I have mentioned, your initial indication to discontinue this study is surprising to us. Would you share with us what point of doctrine it is that troubles you the most?"

At this point the father will normally state a reason for his dissatisfaction. *This first objection given will rarely be the real reason* for withdrawal from his study of the gospel. It is important that the missionaries never enter into a debate to try and prove to the individual that he is wrong and that he should continue to study; rather, they should simply ask, "What else troubles you?" That question should be repeated again and again until the missionary feels certain that the major reason has been expressed or discerned along with the others. With patient understanding, he can then deal with that concern in an objective and spiritual manner. Of course, during the course of these events, the missionaries should be continually praying in their hearts for the power of discernment and for the Holy Spirit to witness and testify to the souls of the family, that they not be lost.

Example One — The Power of the Holy Ghost

When a worthy man hesitates to be baptized and thus is in danger of losing the special blessings that come with that sacred ordinance, the missionary must do all within his power to convince him of his error. On such occasions the missionary could appropriately say to him: "Brother Brown, we understand your concern. In a way, you are telling us that you are like the apostle Peter."

He will probably respond by saying, "What do you mean by that?"

"Well, you remember that Peter was one of the strongest apostles during the ministry of Christ. He was so faithful that he received a vision on a mountain, and he saw Moses, Elias, and Jesus all together. He heard the voice of God testifying that this was Jesus Christ, the Only Begotten. Yet in the emotional stress this strong man suffered at the Savior's arrest he actually denied that he knew him.

"Do you know why that happened to Peter? Had he not received a testimony from God? Surely he had. Then what was he lacking? He lacked the Holy Ghost. Jesus taught his disciples that after he left he would send the Comforter who would teach them all things. In Moroni 10:5 we find that he will tell us the truth of all things.

"It was on the day of Pentecost that Peter received the gift of the Holy Ghost. Never after that did Peter fail in his mission. He was able to suffer affliction and punishment, resist temptations, and, finally, die for the testimony he had received.

"Before he received the Holy Ghost, Peter had been hesitant to comply with the Lord's commandments, even though he had been taught by Christ himself and had heard the voice of God speaking to him from heaven. After the Spirit descended upon him, however, he was strong, carrying the authority of the presidency of the Church and leading the missionary work throughout many nations of the world.

"Now, dear friend, do you believe that you are stronger than Peter? Do you believe that you can go through the trials and temptations of this life alone? Do you believe that you can do what Peter could not do? You are fearful . . ." (At this point the missionaries should say exactly what is bothering the investigator, for example:

—of what your family might think or do?

—that your friends will make fun of your decision to be baptized?

—that you would not keep the Word of Wisdom?

—that you would not be able to pay your tithing?

After selecting the appropriate phrase, the missionary should continue.)

"Even though you know the gospel is true, you continue to worry that you may not have the strength to continue with your conviction. We promise you that if you sincerely repent of your sins, you will reach that level which is required of all those who desire baptism. Let's read together what the Lord has stated in the Doctrine and Covenants: 'All those who humble themselves before God, and desire to be baptized, and come forth with broken hearts and contrite spirits, and witness before the church that they have truly repented of all their sins, and are willing to take upon them the name of Jesus Christ, having a determination to serve him to the end, and truly manifest by their works that they have received of the Spirit of Christ unto the remission of their sins, shall be received by baptism into his church.' (D&C 20:37.)

"Brother Brown, we know that the Lord wants you to become worthy and be baptized. It is not he who is placing doubts of your capacity in your mind. Who is it who would most desire that you not be baptized? Who has the most to gain if you were to remain outside of the kingdom of God? Is it not the adversary?"

At this point the missionaries should, as directed by the Spirit, attempt to establish goals for the investigator to the end that he might become strong and worthy of baptism.

Example Two—The Final Judgment Day

"Brother Brown, we have come to preach the restored gospel because we have a testimony that it is true, that it is important for your future happiness and salvation. It merits sober and careful consideration.

"Someday we may be at the judgment bar of God together. If that occurs, he may say to you, 'Brother Brown, why did you not join my Church? Did you not hear the testimony of my messengers?' Then you would have to answer, 'Yes, I heard it, but . . . '" (At this point the missionary would say that which is bothering the investigator, such as: There was a lot of opposition in my family; I did not want to quit smoking; I did not want to keep the Sabbath day holy; etc.) "Then he probably will ask, 'Do you now believe your reason for not listening to the missionaries was valid? Because you refused the testimony of these missionaries, you also deprived the members of your family of the opportunity to know through you the great truths which were given for your salvation.' The Lord might even ask us, 'Did you not inform this man of his responsibility?' And we would have to say, 'Yes, Lord, we did. We gave him a true testimony.'

"Now, Brother Brown, we testify again that the message we have left you is true; we bear our testimonies to you, but we cannot give you a testimony. You must gain your own testimony, and it will only come to you through study and humble prayer. We say again, if the Lord tells you that you should not be baptized, we will be content to accept the decision. But if after we pray today you have the surety that what we have said is true, then even if it is a sacrifice for you, we hope that as an honest man, you will put your life in order and be baptized for the remission of your sins and make covenants with the Lord to enter into his kingdom."

The missionaries then kneel, signaling to the others present that what they have said was given in humility and solemnity and that they believe the Lord will, in that very moment, confirm the truthfulness of their words.

The procedure is not intended to pressure unworthy investigators to be baptized. It is intended to bring back to the fold a sincere investigator who has been momentarily distracted by unholy influences. The missionaries should use care and discrimination in how the message is presented to insure that the intent is indeed fulfilled.

How to Drop a Family

There are investigator families who truly are not interested in the gospel of Jesus Christ but do enjoy the missionaries' visits. These families are generally identifiable because they do not: 1) study the materials left by the missionaries, 2) pray, or 3) attend Church. If one or more of these conditions exist, the missionaries should prayerfully consider visiting the family less often, because it may be one of Satan's tricks to cause the missionaries to waste their precious time.

If after careful consideration and humble supplication, the missionaries feel that the family should be eliminated from their list of families which are progressing, the following steps may be taken:

1. With great diplomacy inform the family that, as missionaries,

you will not be able to visit them nearly as often as you have done in the past.

2. Indicate that the major portion of missionary time must be dedicated to the preaching of the gospel to those who are studying, praying, attending Church, and progressing toward baptism. That simple explanation may motivate the family to progress more conscientiously.

3. Express love and genuine concern for the family. Reconfirm that visits will be made as often as possible "to keep in touch with them."

4. Bear fervent testimony of the Book of Mormon, encouraging the family to read, ponder, and pray.

If the family still shows no increased interest, then the missionaries should arrange for members to visit the family to continue to friendship them, thus giving the missionaries more time to find other families to teach.

Many times families will realize that they are lacking the Spirit in their lives and that the influence of our Heavenly Father seemed to be present when the missionaries were coming to their home. Therefore, after an appropriate period of waiting, the missionaries should return to the family to evaluate their spiritual condition and to evaluate their readiness to resume progress toward baptism.

Guidelines for Fellowshipping

To become a member of The Church of Jesus Christ of Latter-day Saints, an investigator must conform his or her life to the principles of the gospel. Often the change in life-style is abrupt, and in some cases it requires a great deal of sacrifice on the part of the convert. (Some are literally disinherited by parents who do not understand the witness of the Spirit. They lose their friends, etc.) While such sacrifices are only a small moment in the eternal perspective, it remains self-evident that unless the members of the Church warmly welcome newly baptized members into full fellowship, it is doubtful that they will remain active. In truth it is required of all members to assist in the building up of the kingdom by friendshipping and fellowshipping those who are studying the gospel and those who have joined the Church.

Logically, the member is primarily responsible for this labor, leaving the missionary free to dedicate his time and talents to teaching the gospel. In practice, however, the work is more usually shared, with the missionary also concentrating his efforts on friendshipping and often coordinating the member's effort to do the same.

The concept of fellowshipping is not new. There are many easily identifiable references to this labor in ancient and modern revelation. The Lord has spoken through his servants on this issue on various occasions. Clearly, fellowshipping is established Church practice and reflects our Father's desires that this work be done to assist the convert in making the "social transition" of joining the kingdom.

In keeping the commandments of our Heavenly Father, the convert soon recognizes the importance of not being "of the world." That recognition often provokes change of friends, social customs, Sabbath day activities, and moral responsibilities. These changes can be greatly facilitated if each change becomes an exchange for something better. Changing friends, for example, is not as painful if the new friend is more faithful, helpful, caring, loving, kind, and considerate than the previous one was. The key is to provide plenty of good member friends for the investigators before they are baptized, so that friendships may continue on long after.

The missionaries must lead and coordinate those activities that bring about the proper social transition. The normal procedure is for the missionaries to present the names of their investigator families in the missionary correlation committee meeting. There, assignments are made for members to visit and fellowship each of these families.

Although the assignments are made, the actual visits often fail to take place unless the missionaries assist the members in accomplishing their assignments. The missionary who takes the time to teach members through example the fundamental process of friendshipping is saving time. Once trained, the dedicated member-missionary is a valuable contribution to the missionary effort. Missionaries should never let an opportunity pass by to "teach" members basic friendshipping principles in the meeting-house. Investigators as well as members will always attend church as long as they feel more rewarded for having attended than they do for having stayed away. Members, therefore, should be warm and friendly—anything less may make an investigator feel unwanted. It is a simple matter for missionaries to invite a member to warmly greet investigators or recent converts, to sit with them in the meetings, or help them follow in the hymnbook. Such a demonstration of love and friendship has tremendous impact upon the investigator and, in addition, makes the member feel good.

Many times new members are not assimilated into the ranks of the members as quickly as is desirable. This often results in the inactivity of the recently baptized families. When such a condition occurs, the missionaries should continue to work with the convert families and to help the branch draw them into the fold.

To accomplish this task efficiently, missionaries often hold a weekly fireside chat or a "family" home evening (on some night other than Monday) for recent converts and investigators. The meetings may be held at the Church or in one of the member's homes and are intended to promote social integration and the transition from the old way of life to the new. In this meeting it is appropriate to play games and enjoy one another's company, but the evening should close on a spiritual note, such as brief testimonies from some of the participants. Ward officials should also be invited so they can view the support the missionaries are rendering and can facilitate the final integration into the ward or branch unit.

Whenever possible the missionaries should arrange in advance for the ward members to friendship the convert and one of them to baptize him. If this is done, a bond of brotherhood will be formed between those two people. Fellowshipping takes place as normally and naturally as could ever be expected. As soon as possible the prudent missionary will ask a recent male convert to baptize an investigator convert. In order for this to take place, the missionaries must arrange for the convert to meet the investigator early in the teaching process. The rewards of such efforts are obviously well worth the time spent.

Chapter 16

Guidelines for Mission Leaders

Leadership is an elusive characteristic. At times it would appear to require firmness and at other times, quiet understanding. Both qualities reflect the method of persuasion used by the leader to guide those with whom he works. The unique difference between the manner of leadership used in the world and that used in God's kingdom relates to the concept that the leader is the servant of those he leads and therefore does not view them as subordinates. Further, his leadership calling normally is temporary. Today one missionary is assigned to the task of being the zone leader. After an appropriate period of time, however, he once again may enter the ranks of the proselyting missionaries without additional title or responsibility, and another will take his vacated position. The kingdom is established in that very fashion—to the end that we learn from one another and are all edified.

If that concept is misunderstood and any degree of unrighteousness is exercised, the heavens will withdraw their support. And without that support the missionary will fail to reach his potential. On the other hand, if the newly called leader recognizes that he is to *serve* others and to exercise righteous authority rather than to dominate, he will be magnified in his assignment and blessed for his endeavors.

There is no substitute for success in the Lord's kingdom. This seemingly obvious concept is often ignored. When success is evasive, the careless missionary is lulled subtly to seek substitutes for success. Some missionaries excuse their lack of success all too quickly under the often repeated statement, "This is a hard mission." Others substitute physical work in exchange for convert success. Too often the number of hours worked becomes the desired end result, as the missionary tries to prove to everyone from companion to mission president that in spite of overwhelming odds he is fighting valiantly on to the end of the mission without experiencing baptismal success. For example, many times missionaries schedule visits in a disorganized fashion, necessitating cross-town travel at record speeds and back again, with equal time pressures nipping at their heels both ways, so that they will feel totally "busy" in the Lord's work. We confuse being busy with accomplishing something.

The preceding statements are not meant to stimulate criticism of the faithful and the valiant. Rather, they are intended to identify a common inappropriate practice. "The substitute syndrome," as it may be referred to, can be identified in virtually every mission in the world. It is more prevalent than the common cold, more subtle than a soft breeze, and more weakening than a severed vein. The cure is simply to use one's time more efficiently, and in so doing have greater success. The missionary must always regard true indicators of success as irreplaceable.

If the success concept can be established firmly in the mind and heart of every missionary, then baptisms will be forthcoming. While it is true that some missions have more baptisms than others, it is also true that the missionary who continually seeks to find, teach, and baptize converts into the Church and allows no other goal to replace or alter his course will find success at a higher level than those who do not. He will identify ways to effectively and efficiently find, teach, and baptize converts, because anything less is not in accord with his actions. Success only fails to become his when he loses his efficiency, deviates from his path, or fails to seek divine and mortal help.

The true indicator and constant focal point continues to be the convert who remains active in the Church. If in a mission 20 percent of the missionaries baptize every month with a high retention rate, this is conclusive evidence that it can be done. Armed with that information, the goal is to then eliminate, little by little, the monthly "zero baptizers." If all missionaries develop the positive attitude of everyone baptizing every month, then the program is launched. When a pair of missionaries have reached their monthly goal, they should immediately think of ways to help other missionaries do the same. A cooperative attitude instead of a competitive attitude prevails, and a spirit of love and harmony soon develops.

Each mission leader should review his missionaries on a weekly basis to identify those who are not having success. Once they are identified, the task becomes one of identifying the reasons for their lack of success. The zone leader, the district leader, and even the individual missionary contribute to this analysis. Once a particular weakness has been identified, appropriate training can take place in district and zone training sessions or through companionship splits, with the training missionary being a specialist in the identified area of weakness.

Mission leaders soon learn that missionaries who are baptizing regularly very rarely have companionship or other serious problems. One key to success is to allow the strong missionary to assist the weak, so that the weak may be lifted up and success can take place. Often the scriptural reference for this suggestion, Doctrine and Covenants 84:106, is interpreted to refer only to the spirituality of the individual, but in missionary work it can also be appropriately applied to the skills of a missionary. For example, if a missionary is having difficulty challenging, he should work temporarily with a companion who is experienced and well trained in that area. He will soon "be lifted up" and will be able to successfully and fearlessly challenge the Lord's elect to be baptized.

Clearly, such a process takes place when the mission leaders know the strengths and weaknesses of each missionary. Since that process is dynamic and ever changing, it is important that, if possible, each zone and district leader review weekly each pair of missionaries. As the weaknesses of each missionary are identified and conquered through proper training, one more zero baptizer is eliminated and one more missionary experiences success. The mission moves forward because each missionary is a little more worthy and a little better trained than he was before. The secret of missionary success is tied up in these two basic elements—to be worthy and to be skilled.

As a mission succeeds and a high percentage of the missionaries baptize every month, the goal is changed. If 20 percent of the missionaries are baptizing once every other week, this again is proof that it can be done. The process continues in order to assist every missionary in baptizing every other week. As soon as the mission reaches that level, the next goal, of course, is to baptize every week, and so on.

Zone and District Leaders

In addition to the basic understanding cited above, there are some important operational guidelines which, if heeded, will assist the new zone or district leader. These are:

1. *Be an example in word and deed.* The first task required of a leader is to find, teach, and baptize as many (or more) converts than the other missionaries for whom he is responsible. If the leader is not capable of accomplishing that goal, then he must hurry and become qualified as soon as possible. If he fails in this task, his credibility will suffer. His missionaries will politely listen to his counsel but little else will result from his leadership. He would do well to establish a high baptismal level as his first priority and then maintain that level of performance for the length of his tenure as district or zone leader. It is doubtful that there is a guideline more important.

2. *Show how; don't tell how.* This is an extension of the concept referred to in number one. Some new leaders have a tendency to want to describe how to do a particular task. In a working situation the experienced missionary will show how by his example. In a classroom teaching situation he will draw all of the ideas from the group and give emphasis to the good ideas.

3. *Be slow to judge, quick to praise.* Leaders often feel the necessity to "shape up" their missionaries. They note their faults and with an overabundance of authority initiate corrective measures. Often these distasteful meetings take place in a group

so that unnecessary embarrassment and hurt feelings result. No criticism should be given to any missionary in front of anyone else. If the Spirit directs a reproof, let it be done quietly and privately with the wayward missionary, "then showing forth afterwards an increase of love toward him whom thou hast reproved, lest he esteem thee to be his enemy." (D&C 121:43.)

In addition, every leader should keep in mind that no form of discipline will ever be productive or accepted if the district or zone leader is not living the letter and the spirit of the rules.

4. *Be of service.* The new district or zone leader will soon become aware of the needs of his missionaries. Without being asked, he should render service, satisfying their basic needs. For example, if a missionary is homesick, if there is no hot water in his living quarters, if someone receives his "Dear John" letter, the district leader should be actively engaged in "caring" for these needs. To do so, the leader will often have to sacrifice his time. Except in· emergency situations, he will try to arrange that service to his missionaries is given in time that is not prime proselyting time. He must use his time and energies wisely.

5. *Analyze missionaries' strengths and weaknesses.* If a companionship is not baptizing, it is the responsibility of the leader to identify why and initiate corrective measures. This particular guideline will test the interpersonal relationship skills of the leader. For example, he may find that two missionaries are able to find investigators easily, but they have relatively few baptisms. Since both elders are spiritual and obedient, the leader is left with the option that they either lack teaching skills or they do not know how to properly prepare and challenge their families. The leader further understands that this is a very sensitive issue to both members of that companionship. To directly suggest that they may lack skills in teaching or challenging their investigators may result in two offended, defensive missionaries. What should a leader do if faced with that condition?

There are several alternatives. He could:

—Quietly inform the mission president so that the latter's inspiration may be brought to bear on the case.

—Arrange some district "splits" with other missionaries which would allow an experienced, proven missionary to

visit and teach (challenge) some of the investigator families
of the troubled companionship. (If one member of that
companionship sees the proper example, he will learn and
in turn teach the other missionary.)

—Arrange for some appropriate role-play situations designed
to assist the missionaries in overcoming that particular
weakness. This could be done in a district meeting.

There are many other possible solutions to this problem. The
point is simply that it is the leader's responsibility to analyze
each situation and design a solution to the problem. A leader
will know that he has succeeded when missionaries come to him,
openly describe their proselyting problem, and ask for his advice.
At that point he will know that he has been accepted.

Because the job description for the assistant to the president
varies from mission to mission, there will be no attempt to
develop guidelines for that position; however, those *principles*
relative to leadership positions mentioned herein are also trans-
ferable to other positions, such as assistant to the president.

Missionary Trainers

The profound influence of a missionary's first companion,
good or bad, cannot be underestimated. All missionaries remember their first companion, because it is he who deals with all of
the expectations and needs of the newly arrived missionary and
through example or word drafts for him an explanation of what
the mission really is. Since the new missionary has rarely had
other valid missionary experiences, he generally accepts at face
value that which his companion states as being accurate and sets
his course accordingly. If the training missionary misses the
mark, the trainee will follow, emulating the same attitudes, forms
of teaching, biases, desires, and work habits. If the trainer suggests that the mission is a hard mission and low in baptisms,
thus it is. On the other hand, if the trainer suggests a positive
attitude the trainee will likely express the same.

Any missionary who is called to be a trainer should seriously
contemplate the responsibility which is his, for no other assignment in missionary work can influence the life of one missionary
so directly or with such lasting influence as that of a trainer.

Because of the obvious ramifications of his efforts, a training missionary would do well to consider the following guidelines to help his companion become a well-adjusted and productive missionary:

1. *Express love unfeigned.* The adage that people do not care how much one knows until they know how much one cares is true. It is important to consistently demonstrate love for the newly arrived companion, and concern relative to his progress as a missionary and as an individual. For example, should his companion wish to sleep in until 9 A.M., the trainer has an immediate problem to solve. If every problem, regardless of what it is, is addressed in a spirit of true love, so that the trainee truly understands that the advice is given because the trainer loves him and is genuinely interested in his personal growth and progress, then there will be very few barriers between companions which will be too high to cross.

2. *Establish correct priorities.* Each missionary comes into the field with his or her own personal desires. Many times these desires are incompatible with that which should have higher priority. In such cases the trainer is responsible to help the new missionary ferret out his goals and give them appropriate priority. For example, new missionaries often arrive in the field desirous of sending their new address to their friends and relatives and are less desirous of studying the missionary discussions. The priorities are backwards. It is the task of the trainer, with tact and love, to sit down with his companion and through proper planning of the missionary work establish proper sequence and priorities.

3. *Be true to the rules.* If the trainer demonstrates through his actions the importance of rules, there will rarely be a problem with a new missionary's keeping them. Getting up on time, going out to work on time, having daily discussion review, offering prayers, and many more practices are a way of life for missionaries. If the trainer organizes each day so there are scheduled times to accommodate these activities, then his example in doing them according to the letter and spirit of the rule will virtually disclaim any need for discussion regarding their appropriateness. The trainer's example is sufficient.

4. *Help the missionary to learn the discussions well.* If there is

one bench mark of success in the new missionary's progress, it is in passing off all of his discussions. In planning sessions the trainer should emphasize the importance of reaching that goal and suggest a format of how he can assist. For example:

- Identify how many lines can be learned per hour and then per day. Then jointly set appropriate goals.
- Make adequate time available for the exclusive memorization of the discussions.
- Suggest to the new missionary that he signal when he becomes tired and his mind starts to wander. When this point is reached, the trainer can sit with him, ask him relevant questions regarding the material being learned, and in other ways render support so that the learning process can continue.
- Volunteer to do all cooking and dishwashing so that the new missionary may have more time to study.

There are other guidelines which might be given, but experience has proven these four to be of significant importance. If these four principles are followed carefully, they will be of immense value to the trainer as he prayerfully seeks guidance from the Spirit in helping his companion adjust and become a more effective missionary.

Senior Companions

The two major challenges for the senior companion are: first, to recognize that it is his responsibility to train and develop his companion's spirituality and missionary technique; and second, to capitalize on the strengths, ideas, talents, and spiritual gifts of his companion. Often senior companions falsely assume that because they have been assigned as senior companion, all direction rests with them, that it is the junior companion's role to listen and follow without question. Few senior companions catch the entire view of their role as a trainer, friend, and brother.

In proper perspective the senior companion would be well advised to consider his own role to be "senior servant" in charge of coordinating good ideas from his junior companion with ideas of his own. "Sharing and caring" should be his motto and his charge—to magnify his companion's talents and gifts to the end that he becomes an effective teacher of righteousness and a leader in the Lord's kingdom. Serve. Do not command. Lead by example.

The mission field is an appropriate training ground for life. With that concept in mind, the following general guidelines to senior companions are presented:

1. *Be a trainer, not a dictator.* Successful leaders carefully measure their responsibilities instead of their power.

> We have learned by sad experience that it is the nature and disposition of almost all men, as soon as they get a little authority, as they suppose, they will immediately begin to exercise unrighteous dominion. (D&C 121:39.)

The power of a senior companion rests totally in his ability to serve. To serve well, he must first identify what needs to be done, and second, attend to it in a fitting manner. For him to properly identify what he needs to do is not difficult. A sensitive senior companion will soon note in his companion those areas which need improvement if he is going to be an effective missionary. If the junior companion lacks technical skills in asking golden questions, for example, the senior companion should organize nonthreatening role-play situations in their apartment— with follow-up practice with members until the junior companion is totally trained in that particular skill and feels confident. Little by little each additional precept and skill is patiently taught, first by example and then by practice, until the junior companion becomes self-assured and capable.

2. *Delegate responsibility.* A good leader delegates his responsibility as much as possible to those who are under his direction. The senior companion who follows this guideline will increase the level of respect afforded him, he will become more efficient, and he will help his companion grow and develop. When the leader learns to delegate, the weight of responsibility is then shared between companions. The counsel given to Moses by his father-in-law is representative of the concept under consideration:

And it came to pass on the morrow, that Moses sat to judge the people: and the people stood by Moses from the morning unto the evening.

And when Moses' father in law saw all that he did to the people, he said, What is this thing that thou doest to the people? why sittest thou thyself alone, and all the people stand by thee from morning unto even?

And Moses said unto his father in law, Because the people come unto me to enquire of God:

When they have a matter, they come unto me; and I judge between one and another, and I do make them know the statutes of God, and his laws.

And Moses' father in law said unto him, The thing that thou doest is not good.

Thou wilt surely wear away, both thou, and this people that is with thee: for this thing is too heavy for thee; thou art not able to perform it thyself alone. (Exodus 18:13-18.)

The senior companion should not try to carry the full burden alone. There is too much to accomplish. Not unlike Moses of old, unless the senior companion delegates some of the work, he will "surely wear away." The actual process of deciding the division of labor between companions evolves as they mutually discuss elements of the work. Unitedly they reach agreement as to who should do what. The process is a joint sharing of ideas and a contributing of spirit, talents, and desires to do the Lord's work.

3. *Be an example.* While the Prophet was suffering in Liberty Jail, he cried out to the Lord asking how long he would have to suffer. The Lord said:

And if thou shouldst be cast into the pit, or into the hands of murderers, and the sentence of death passed upon thee; if thou be cast into the deep; if the billowing surge conspire against thee; if fierce winds become thine enemy; if the heavens gather blackness, and all the elements combine to hedge up the way; and above all, if the very jaws of hell shall gape open the mouth wide after thee, know thou, my son, that all these things shall give thee experience, and shall be for thy good.

The Son of Man hath descended below them all. Art thou greater than he? (D&C 122:7-8; emphasis added.)

What greater example could the Savior have given than that which is here penned? "The Son of Man hath descended below them all." He was the perfect example; there is none greater. The message is clear: If the missionary would be properly trained, the senior companion must be the example. In so being, he makes proper training takes place naturally and automatically.

The senior companion should be the model by obeying *all* rules of the mission, be an example in his studies and knowledge of the discussions and scriptures, be an example for his companion in his prayers, be careful never to require his companion to do that which he himself would not do or has not done, and be enthusiastic about missionary work by using his imagination and talents. Through example he should teach his companion the missionary skills that will help him to become an effective senior companion. In essence, the senior companion should strive to be the model missionary.

Chapter 17

The Urgency of the Work

The Doctrine and Covenants declares the degree of suffering which is the inevitable consequence of unrepented sins.

> Therefore I command you to repent—repent, lest I smite you by the rod of my mouth, and by my wrath, and by my anger, and your sufferings be sore—how sore you know not, how exquisite you know not, yea, how hard to bear you know not.
> For behold, I, God, have suffered these things for all, that they might not suffer if they would repent. (D&C 19:15-16.)

In these two short sentences the Lord uses the word *repent* three times. Clearly, those who are called to the work are to cry repentance. It is the Lord's commandment. Through the above expression we can better understand the great importance and urgency of missionary work. The people of the world will not have to suffer if they will but accept the gospel and repent.

The Lord continued:

> But if they would not repent *they must suffer even as I;*
> Which suffering caused myself, even God, the greatest of all, to tremble because of pain, and to bleed at every pore, and to suffer both body and spirit. (D&C 19:17-18; emphasis added.)

If missionaries could realize the intense suffering that takes place in the body and spirit of the unrepentant sinner, and if that concept could but reach the center of their understanding, how much more diligent they would be in their labors!

Elder W. Grant Bangerter tells of a missionary in Brazil who was greeted at a door by the maid. She proceeded to tell the missionaries that the lady of the house was not home. The missionary responded, "Young lady, why did you just lie to us? Don't you know that we are representatives of the Lord Jesus Christ? We know that the lady of the house is in, because we saw her through the window as we approached the door. Please tell her that we are here in her best interests and have an important message for her. And," he concluded, "don't lie again to messengers of our Heavenly Father." (Mission Presidents Seminar, Provo, Utah, 1980.)

That missionary had the vision of the importance of his role. It did not trouble him that the lady had probably instructed the maid to say that she was not in. His message was more important than anything else that she might have planned, and this he knew. Many missionaries would have immediately left, counting her actions as sufficient enough to condemn her. Personally offended, they might say, "Why waste time on someone like that when the Lord has his elect who are waiting?" The missionary who is offended because of such treatment has not yet reached the level of understanding and maturity that is needed in the mission field. Missionaries must overlook such discourtesies and go to the heart of the issue—the salvation of the individual and his eternal happiness.

The Prophet Joseph Smith taught:

> Happiness is the object and design of our existence; and will be the end thereof, if we pursue the path that leads to it. (Joseph Smith, *Teachings of the Prophet Joseph Smith*, sel. Joseph Fielding Smith [Salt Lake City: Deseret Book Company, 1938], p. 255.)

The missionary has a sobering responsibility. Somehow, he must help the investigator realize that it is his to choose—the profound depths of suffering that come to all unrepentant sinners, or celestial joy and happiness for those who will but repent. The contrast is literal. It is complex in that man cannot comprehend the level of suffering which comes to those who do not repent. We mortals have little point of reference for such depth of pain. We can only weakly relate to those earthly trials which have brought us sorrow and humbly try to understand the suffering of the unrepentant sinner.

When I was but a boy, I had a little white dog with black spots named Skippy. He had all of the attributes of a boy's perfect dog. He was my constant companion. I recall how we would roll and tumble on the lawn—me laughing until tears came. He would lick my face and jump on me in the mornings to wake me up. We played together; we slept together; we did everything together. I loved that dog more than anything else in the world, save my own parents.

One day as mother, Skippy, and I were returning from shopping, we were crossing the street when a car turned the corner into our lane. Skippy, who was a few feet ahead of us, was right in the path of the car. There was only a dull thud and a yelp of pain as the car hit him. The next thing I remember, Skippy was dragging his broken body over to where I was. Blood was coming out of his mouth and he was whimpering in excruciating pain. His back was obviously broken, as his hind legs failed to function. He looked up at me in a pitiful way and cried out to me for help. There was nothing I could do. In a matter of minutes Skippy suffered his last pain and died in agony at my feet.

Many, many years have passed by since that incident, and to this day I cannot think of that fateful day without tears welling up in my eyes. I do not remember how many nights, as a little boy, I cried myself to sleep or how many times I prayed asking why Skippy had to be taken.

We can relate to the suffering and death of a little dog. Why should we not be able to relate to the suffering, pain, and anguish that will come in an incomprehensible degree to the unrepentant sinner? Should we be less sympathetic to the suffering of a brother or sister than to a dog? I think not.

If with every contact the missionary mentally visualizes that person suffering in "both body and spirit" at a future time unless repentance takes place, he might begin to sense the importance of the delivery of his divine message. He must understand that the message of the gospel, if spiritually listened to, can prevent inexplicable pain and suffering. Those missionaries who can visualize their contacts gaining inexplicable joy through baptism and obedience to God's law are armed with added comprehension and are able to bear a stronger witness and a bolder testimony.

The task is for every missionary to catch the vision of the urgency and importance of this message. Each must realize that the literal salvation of many depends upon the missionary's ability to comprehend the importance and urgency of his message. If this is understood, that missionary will have additional desire and motivation to properly prepare himself in terms both of worthiness and of understanding of the principles of effective proselyting. He thus can become a true missionary of the Lord Jesus Christ to go fearlessly forth to preach the gospel unto the salvation of all who would give heed to his words.

Index